Follow Your Heart to Discover Your Life Purpose

Follow Your Heart
to Discover Your Life Purpose

*A Guide to Creating Authenticity in Your
Relationships, Career, and Health and Wellness*

Kelly MacLellan, M.Sc.

iUniverse, Inc.
Bloomington

Follow Your Heart to Discover Your Life Purpose
A Guide to Creating Authenticity in Your Relationships, Career, and Health and Wellness

Disclaimer: The stories used in this book are true, but all names and some identifying details have been changed to protect the privacy of the individuals involved. The reader takes all responsibility for his/her use of the material written in the book. This book intends to educate and teach people self-exploration tools to assist in leading more meaningful lives. The result of using these techniques may vary, depending on how they are used.

The views and advice expressed in this book are not intended to be a substitute for conventional counseling services. If you have any concern regarding your mental health, consult with a professional counselor in your local area.

iUniverse books may be ordered through booksellers or by contacting:

iUniverse
1663 Liberty Drive
Bloomington, IN 47403
www.iuniverse.com
1-800-Authors (1-800-288-4677)

Because of the dynamic nature of the Internet, any web addresses or links contained in this book may have changed since publication and may no longer be valid. The views expressed in this work are solely those of the author and do not necessarily reflect the views of the publisher, and the publisher hereby disclaims any responsibility for them.

Any people depicted in stock imagery provided by Thinkstock are models, and such images are being used for illustrative purposes only.
Certain stock imagery © Thinkstock.

ISBN: 978-1-4620-6365-9 (sc)
ISBN: 978-1-4620-6367-3 (hc)
ISBN: 978-1-4620-6366-6 (e)

Printed in the United States of America
iUniverse rev. date: 11/08/2011

Contents

Acknowledgments

In life, we never work alone.

I want to take this opportunity to express my love, gratitude, and respect to those who have touched my life.

To begin, I am humbled and deeply grateful to the universal God and all of the other heavenly beings that guide me every day. On the darkest of days and during times of joyful celebration, I feel your presence and love.

To my amazing and dedicated clients, you continue to achieve your goals, persevering and keeping your sights on what you want! Your energy inspires me to continually grow and approach my work passionately. It has been an honor to work with each of you.

To the children at Café con Leche in the Dominican Republic, each of you with your shining, smiling, happy faces healed my heart. I arrived to give, and you gave me so much more. When I think of you, life sparkles.

To all of the yoga instructors, professors, massage therapists, writing and spiritual teachers, and authors who have influenced my life perspectives that helped to uncover my current level of truth—

because you dare to open your hearts and share your message with the world, I am daring to share mine.

To my friends and family, especially my parents and our dog, Chloe, your loyalty, love, and support are my dearest blessings. You provide me with treasured memories and promising future adventures.

To my husband and daughter, I waited for you for so long. When it was time, you entered my life. You teach me how much more I am capable of. Because of you, my light shines brighter. I love you.

Warmest Greetings and Overview

I believe that books find us when we are ready for them, like the old adage, "When the student is ready, the teacher will appear." Here we are, our paths intersecting.

It is very likely that you are scanning titles and outlines looking for an answer to solve a problem in your life. You may find what you are looking for in one paragraph, or the entire book may captivate and inspire you. Whatever happens, I am honored to be a part of your journey.

I present to you these words and ideas from my heart and hold the intention that they resonate with you, energize you, and inspire you at a heart level to believe in your dreams and yourself. I speak to those people who have given up hope or have lost themselves in the busyness of life. I want to remind you that all is possible and there is a way back to your true path. While you learn to open your heart and trust your voice, I encourage you to return to this book for guidance and inspiration. You can get out of your situation, life can be good, and you can be happy.

First, this is a workbook, and like the word suggests, some work is required. Many of us would agree that it would be wonderful to reap the benefits of someone else doing our exercise for us, but this is simply impossible. We must do our own sit-ups to have a flat, strong stomach and therefore must also do our own self-exploration.

The benefits of completing this work are life-transforming and fulfilling. It is impossible to be the same when you have learned something new. You will see things differently, including yourself, your environment, and what you are capable of achieving. You will see again that it is possible to hope and believe in your dreams.

With the intention of encouraging ease of self-exploration, there is a journal section contained within this book. The journal section can be found in the back pages of this book for the purpose of capturing the ideas, insights, and inspirations you come across as you are open to the possibilities presented to you along your journey.

However, before you begin to transform your life and live out your dream, let's step back from what's troubling you, examine what currently isn't working, and identify what you want to change.

Generally, *we all want to be happy and live meaningful lives.* But what makes us happy? How do we live meaningfully? These do not have to be difficult questions to answer, and I hope to provide insight and inspiration within this resource. The answers form once we have uncovered what we want to change; from here, we then have the room to begin to dream and create pictures of what we want ideally. Therefore, your dreams form your ideal pictures, which will serve as motivation for present behavior and guide you as you make choices throughout each day. Your ideal pictures will be created by clarifying and understanding what you ideally want.

> We've got to have a dream if we are going to make a dream come true.
>
> —Denis Waitley

My professional expertise is coaching people to discover their life purpose and create meaningful life and career action plans. When we are clear about our purpose for living, our careers as well as our relationships and health improve.

In order to best present the material within this book, I have decided to categorize life into three main areas: relationships, career, and health and wellness. However, if there are things you would like to change that do not necessarily fall within these categories, please write these down too.

The Follow Your Heart program has seven steps that represent each chapter of this book:

1. Identify What You Want to Change
2. Create a Picture of Your Life Purpose
3. Begin to Live Your Life Purpose
4. Protect Your Ideal Picture
5. Be in the Moment
6. Realign with Your Life Purpose!
7. Continue to Evolve

You may ask yourself these questions:

I have tried to change in the past. Why should I keep trying?

The answer is that if you don't discover your life purpose and live accordingly, there will always be a part of you that is searching, yearning, and daydreaming—thinking, *What if?* It is human nature to strive to fulfill our life purpose. We will continue to search for meaning until we begin listening to the messages leading us and believing in the dreams that live in our hearts.

Okay, but how is this time going to be different?

When we recognize our power, we become empowered. Fear is the main thing holding us back from living our purpose and using our power. Whenever we doubt ourselves, our intuition, or our hearts, fear quickly takes over, paralyzing our growth. Fear drives us back to our familiar place even if it is unsatisfactory and uncomfortable. We endure these circumstances because it is safer than facing the unknown. Read the following typical scenarios. Have any of these happened to you?

Scenario 1: Your goal is to have a healthier lifestyle. It is January, and this is your New Year's resolution. You begin to lose weight by going to the gym regularly and participating in a new exercise class and are seeing the effects in your life. It is exciting! By February, you feel confident in your progress and reward yourself by taking a day off here and there. Slowly, one by one, the old habits come back, and you begin to make promises to yourself to get back to the gym, but it never happens. Feelings of guilt enter your mind.

Scenario 2: Your goal is to create more positive, uplifting relationships. In accordance with this goal, you decide to end a friendship or relationship that is draining you. Wow! Great work! You know it was the right decision, and you are very proud of yourself. You feel strong and ready to attract an ideal mate and have more quality friendships. Things are quiet, and you haven't met anyone new. Doubt slowly creeps in and overtakes your thoughts, and you quickly accept some of the unacceptable behaviors again from those around you to avoid being alone. Then the patterns begin again.

Scenario 3: Your goal is to change your job, go back to school, or pursue a new career entirely. Everyone thinks you are wrong for changing directions and leaving the security of your last job, especially in this job market. But you go forward instead and make the change. You feel great! But after a few months, this restless feeling arises, and you begin to yearn for something different. You feel guilty for always changing and wanting more. It seems like you will never find what you are looking for.

It is going to be different this time because you know what is stopping you: fear. In all three scenarios, you have an idea of what you want and how to get it, and while you start the process and make *huge* changes in your life, you lose the momentum or direction and give up. Doubt, fear, and critical voices quickly enter in and overwhelm you, creating excuses for you to protect yourself.

This workbook will help keep the momentum going when fear approaches. We will get clear about the purpose of why we are pursuing goals so they are meaningful when we achieve them.

We will examine and let go of old and deeply held beliefs and form new ones that are consciously created and more effective. We will strengthen your spiritual connection to Source, attracting power from the universe to develop your intuition.

You will learn to listen and open your heart, thus being able to receive what is waiting to enter your life. You will learn to set clear intentions and live your life purpose by relying on your heart for direction and using your inner voice to speak your truth to others.

Your world will open up, and you will have the tools to overcome any fear that enters your life story. Fear is replaced with love. You will live powerfully, clearly, authentically, and purposefully in the world.

How to Benefit from This Book

How many self-help books do you have in your house? How many do you think you have read in your entire life? How many have you finished or promised yourself you would finish? Think about your piles of books now. Do you think you have learned anything from these books? Which books have impacted or inspired you?

The books I have benefitted from the most have been the ones where I have actually completed the recommended exercises and activities. It is not knowledge alone that changes our lives but the application of that knowledge. Therefore, I recommend that you complete each activity and exercise to get the most from this experience.

There are a few essential practices that I will speak of throughout this book: writing, yoga and meditation, walking in nature, and having accountability. Each practice cultivates our relationship with God. Each can be considered a form of prayer as we immerse ourselves in activities that develop our connection with ourselves and God, Divinity, Source, the Universe. Through these practices, we can access spiritual and helpful guidance.

Writing
The first essential practice I recommend is that you commit to writing daily in a journal. In addition to the area found within this book, your journal could be kept on your computer, or you can use the old-fashioned pen and paper method.

"Ewww, journaling," some of you may say. Let me point out that there are so many reasons to begin to capture your feelings and thoughts in writing.

Number one is that writing is a release; you do not need to carry these words around with you all day. The voices that persist and keep you distracted from reality need to be released for you to gain clarity in your day-to-day behavior. Think of a to-do list. Who wants to spend hours thinking about not forgetting to buy the milk? Just write it down and get on with your day. You can keep your thoughts all in one place, and you can visit them, if you choose, whenever you want. Writing creates a new level of self-awareness and a technique for letting go of fear.

One of my clients writes her thoughts in a word-processing program and e-mails them daily to me. She finds that the action of writing and then releasing when she pushes the send button is a healing process resulting in her feeling lighter and more positive as she approaches each day.

When you write, you are making a conscious choice to create time and space for self-development. You are sending out the message to everyone, including yourself, that this is you-time, and it is important. This special time alone can be very therapeutic. It can be a time for listening to what you are thinking and feeling, what your desires are, and what troublesome situations are draining your energy. Writing every day, even a little, is a healthy, accessible way to practice self-care and develop our intuition.

Writing also serves as a record of your progress, reflections, releases, and insightful, aha moments! All of this serves as a wonderful reminder of how far you have come once you embarked on this experience.

If you are ever stumped about what to write, don't fret. This book is a hands-on, practical tool to help you get in touch with your thoughts. I will be asking you to consider many questions that will trigger thoughtful responses. The journal section contained within this book is a convenient place for you to capture and record any new shifts in your awareness about an issue, problem, or situation that arises.

Also, everyone's writing style is different. There is no right way to write, just your way. You do not need to write pages and pages. If you feel more comfortable scribbling a few words or just creating lists, that works! The way you express yourself is entirely up to you. No one will read this unless you share it!

And for those of you who are nervous about privacy, there is a sneaky way to maintain your anonymity. Create an e-mail account that is your pen name (any name you want), write your thoughts in an e-mail, and send them to that account.

Yoga and Meditation
The second essential practice of this program is to engage in daily yoga and meditation, ideally in the morning. A yoga mat or comfortable rug is all the equipment needed for this essential element of the program. If you are not familiar with either yoga or meditation, I have posted on my website at www.embraceyourlife. ca basic instructions on how to do sun salutations and how to meditate. Also, there are many instructional videos and yoga classes that you can research online and in your community. The important thing is to find the best fit for you. In the resource section of this book, there is a list of resources, including books and websites that might be helpful in taking your next step toward incorporating yoga and meditation in your daily routine.

Participating in gentle hatha yoga postures followed by fifteen minutes of meditation will radically shift your approach to one of mindfulness. We will speak more fully about mindfulness later in this book. Those willing to commit additional time and energy will reap greater benefits from this experience.

Walking in Nature
Another essential practice of this program is to walk in nature regularly, paying attention to your perceptions and your senses.

I don't know if the people in my neighborhood witness the time during my daily walks when I put my hand on the same tree and lean back with my arms outstretched and my head to the sky, repeating aloud my mantra: "Goodness is constantly being sent to me. I accept abundance into my life." I know it sounds a bit odd, but this regular practice always makes me smile and giggle afterward. During the day, when faced with challenging situations, I remember touching "my" tree and the way the sky looked that morning and the quietness of my morning walk. It restores my inner peace, and I am centered again. You don't have to talk aloud while touching trees, but if the urge arises, go ahead!

Walking in nature reminds us of our connection with Mother Earth. As we walk, we see flowers, trees, bugs, and even our neighbors! We see things differently. We see things we wouldn't see if we were driving. Getting outside and breathing fresh air helps us slow down and look a little deeper at everything that surrounds us. When we connect with nature, we remember our natural rhythm and are able to cope more effectively with troubles that arise in our lives.

Accountability
Another element that I would highly recommend adding to this program is a way to hold yourself accountable to the goals that you set for yourself. Going through this program with an accountability partner or a professional life coach will help motivate you as you brainstorm and explore new behaviors. By sharing, transporting, and holding each other's visions and intentions, your visions will manifest transformation in your life!

So with that being said, let's get on with it! I am excited! I hope that you are too!

The time has come. Your time to live, to celebrate and see the goodness that you are. Do not fight the dark, just turn on the light. Let go. And breathe into the goodness that you are.

—Swami Kripalu

Follow Your Heart—My Story

Tears spiked to the surface, and I unexpectedly began sobbing. I couldn't stop myself. I excused myself from the table, shocking everyone there, including myself, with my emotional meltdown. Only moments before I was chatting easily with my in-laws, and then the muscles in my neck began getting tighter and my voice got higher. *What am I getting worked up about?* I wondered as my face started to blush deep red. And then all of the sudden, my body began trembling and I started crying.

We were discussing the importance of giving in the community, and I reluctantly shared with the group that I hadn't given of my time recently. This admission felt very uncomfortable, as my entire career had always been working directly serving the public. Up until this point in my life, my motto was always, "Do what you love and the money will follow." And the money did always follow, but something changed when I recently accepted a position not for the love of the work but I admit for the money. I felt trapped.

I began defending myself to the group, but something inside me knew my arguments didn't sit well. I couldn't help but remember my young, ambitious, ideal self and how far removed I was from this woman who existed only a few years earlier. My life was nothing like what I dreamed of when I started out on my own.

Trying to compose myself in the kitchen, I dabbed at my eyes, but when I opened them Kelly, aged twenty-one, sat there, shiny, trusting, and positive, looking back at me. I stared at her. She smiled encouragingly at me, almost knowingly. Feeling strange, I blinked, and when I opened my eyes again, she smiled, and we held our gaze. I looked deeply into her eyes, searching, and saw her effortless beauty. She seemed peaceful and calm; it was as if she glowed. And then the moment passed. I don't know how long it was that I was standing there. I closed my eyes and stood there alone in the kitchen. Finally, I rejoined the others. My tears dried, but my entire body felt hollow and strange. Something had shifted, and the world looked a bit different from this place.

This experience was only one of the numerous episodes that signaled that the truth was getting closer to the surface and my inner voice was getting stronger; it was only a matter of time. But I pushed it down further.

Speaking the truth and following my heart, I believed, would destroy everything I knew, including my marriage, and would hurt a lot of people. Later I realized facing this decision to speak my truth and choose to follow my heart would nearly kill me!

Nearly two years after my meltdown in the kitchen, I was driving on a snowy road on my way to work. My hands gripped the wheel firmly. My eyes and head were blurry. It had been a very depressing day, and it wasn't even 9:00! Earlier that morning, I blankly drank my coffee and sat staring out of the window. I watched children and their parents walk to school. Tears rolled down my face. My heart was broken. The grief was unbearable.

Walking to school is a normal thing to do for most families, something that wouldn't cause such a reaction, but I had had a miscarriage, and over one year later believed that I was infertile. I didn't know it at the time, but I was very depressed.

At every turn, someone was pregnant. Four of the seven women at work were pregnant, and the remaining were already mothers. My cousin was pregnant, and so was my best friend! Even my massage therapist was pregnant, not to mention the baby buzz in the media about celebrity babies! Losing the baby—a phrase I grew to despise—was devastating.

During those few weeks that I was pregnant, we purchased our dream home in the suburbs. This house was supposed to be the perfect setting for my growing family, but after the miscarriage and then the time that passed, I was resigned to the reality that my family wasn't growing. There I sat day after day watching "normal" suburban families live out their days together while my husband and I grew more disconnected, and I grew more depressed every day. That morning was particularly difficult.

Driving slowly down the main street, I questioned aloud whether I was really visible to the outside world. My voice sounded hollow and dark. *Do I even exist? Do people really see me? Is this a horrible dream? Does any of this struggling really matter? I can't leave. I don't want a divorce. I can't live this way anymore. What if I did die? I can't hurt anymore. Would anyone even care?*

Numbly, I turned left onto the snowy road and maneuvered to keep the car in the icy tracks to avoid going off the road. Yet my previous thoughts lingered. *Who cares? What difference would it make anyway?*

I looked at the snow banks on either side of the country road and at my speedometer and realized that I had a choice.

We all have a choice. We all have our own reasons to stay where we are doing what we always do. We stay in dead-end jobs or relationships when we aren't happy even when we know it is time to move on. We face other hardships in our lives, like unemployment, divorce, and illness, struggling to just make it through the day. We focus on the pain, and in doing so, we become depressed, isolated, and angry. We excuse our behavior, pushing away our intuition because we are afraid of the unknown. *It is just easier this way*, we think. However, the sadness and pain manifest in strange ways: our back hurts, we develop migraine headaches, and we experience chronic money problems, anxiety attacks, and so on. We hold onto the old because we are afraid of the new or the unknown.

Professionally, I know this to be true because I have observed my clients, even after experiencing traumatic events, excel in school, overcome language barriers, and even learn to use their non-dominant hands to write, return to work, and generally be happier when they aren't focused on their physical pain. Alternatively, I have witnessed many clients struggling with their pain and getting stuck.

Personally, I know this is true because I lived unfulfilled and in denial for years, and the pain and incongruence manifested in infertility, or so I thought for many years.

It is a common belief that our physical body reflects the quality of our thinking. Experts agree that our thoughts are beyond powerful. They shape our reality. Simply stated, thoughts are measurable units of energy that send a vibration into the world and what you send out comes back to you. When you are afraid and thinking fearful thoughts, your body changes and your heart beats faster. Your thoughts travel faster, and your stress level increases. Alternatively, when you are relaxed and thinking peaceful thoughts, your body changes and your heart beats slower. Your thoughts travel slower, and your stress level decreases. What you attract is more of the same of whatever you are putting out. Therefore, your body reflects the vibrational level of your thoughts and changes your experience in life.

That day in my car while I was driving down that snowy road, I can recall vividly the sorrow and despair that weighed heavily all throughout my body as I faced my options. I pulled over to the side of the road, crying. I let it all go and surrendered to the pain, not able to bear it any longer. I released the pain, and my body felt peaceful, lighter.

What followed, the only way I can describe it, was a flash of insight. White energy surrounded me, and I felt an undeniable clarity. In that one moment, *I refused to live one more day in sadness.* I made the decision to choose happiness and end the struggle.

Numb, cold, and weak, I slowly turned the car around and drove home. I arrived, turned off the phone, walked upstairs to my room, climbed into bed, and pulled the duvet close around me. There were no thoughts, just quietness. I slept for many hours and woke up relieved, soft, and peaceful.

In the many months that followed, the courage to speak and live my truth did surface, and there was no turning back. I talked with my husband, but it was clear how reckless we had been with our marriage. We lost our connection and our trust of one another. My husband and I eventually separated and later divorced after our ten-year relationship, which, as I expected, hurt and shocked people close to us.

My heart still hurts at the grief created by divorce in my life. However, as time and forgiveness heal and my ex-husband and I each continue on our paths, I believe and am comforted to know that we remain to be good people who did our best and are now more self-aware as a result of our relationship. I learned a lot of lessons and continue to learn from this extremely important relationship in my life.

> You can be pleased with nothing when you are not pleased with yourself.
>
> —Lady Mary Wortley Montagu

I Tried So Hard to Be Good!

Before I felt trapped at every turn. I had done everything right, pleased people, and played the "good girl" role. Somewhere in my early development, I picked up the belief that in order to be loved, I had to be good. I felt I had to prove my worth. Nothing I ever accomplished or participated in, including relationships, ever gave me the peace and acceptance I longed and fought for.

Simultaneously, I also held the belief that I shouldn't be "too good" and was able to become unsettlingly "invisible" if the situation required it. I learned this coping strategy when I survived for two years beginning at age twelve, against a group of rough girls who harassed me relentlessly. Because of them, I instinctually looked to others for safety and security but was repeatedly let down.

I played these roles for so long that I couldn't figure out what to do next with my life. I was ready to let go of these old beliefs that limited me. They obviously weren't working!

I was ready at age thirty-one to dare to be me—whoever that was! I replaced those old beliefs formed using flawed information with the quote by Charles Haanel:

> I am whole, perfect, strong, powerful, loving, harmonious and happy!

Then I added, "I am exactly where I am meant to be."

I repeated this affirmation many, many times during each day.

I still didn't know what I was going to do next. All I knew was that I couldn't go back and that I needed to move forward lovingly. I had no idea what I was moving forward to, but I knew there was no other choice.

I began to feel my way through this time of change and transition and knew that I was moving in the right direction. Real change was happening! For so long, I had been determined to create a picture of perfection, but now what was happening was way better than what I could imagine!

Before, I exercised frantically to create the perfect body, but I was heavy and was so defeated by the limited success of the results. There was a difference this time. I felt light. By following my intuition and trusting myself, my body felt great! I no longer pushed myself and the pounds melted away!

Each day as I would bathe or dress, I would examine my body, thanking it for carrying me through my daily experiences in the world. I began loving my legs; this was revolutionary to me, as historically, my legs were the target of distaste about my appearance. I turned it around and said to my legs, *Thank you. You are strong and long and lean.* And eventually they became that way. They really did!

My heart soared when I thought of all of the possibilities I had now, and as a result, newness flowed into my life! My body shifted as a result of this new flow of energy.

Following what was in my heart was not only empowering—it was exhilarating! I didn't have to work so hard. What a concept! I was just doing what made me happy and what felt good. These new thoughts triggered new behaviors and sparked other affirmations that became very familiar, like a favorite blanket that I want to share here with you for inspiration: *I am responsible only to myself,* and *I choose happiness and love.*

I was being me, and finally just being me was enough! I ended the constant struggle of trying to prove myself.

I stopped playing the roles in my life that I thought I had to play. I started becoming aware of how I tried to validate myself and try to prove my worth in my daily interactions. Now when I was in a conversation with someone, when I felt the urge to jump in with a witty comment or joke, I stopped myself and instead let the moment pass. I would ask myself quickly, *Am I trying to get this person to like me more by being funny or smart or wanting them to accept me?* And if I was, I kept my mouth closed. I became a better listener to the person talking and also to my inner voice. I was liberated. I found my voice. I was free!

I was learning how to nurture and trust myself. I began receiving messages that inspired and encouraged me exactly when I needed them. I was drawn to new places, people, and even food. Everything was delicious! Apples were vividly red, sounds were crystal clear, and textures were ... flavorful!

On one occasion, when I was out with my puppy, Chloe, we discovered a nearby forested area. We walked along a trail through the woods on a mild winter day. It was one of those gorgeous days when the sky was a crisp, clear blue, and the yellow rays beamed brightly off the snow, making everything seem shimmery like diamonds. Quietly we crunched through the snow and slowly made our way down a hill. We stopped at the bottom and stood there listening to the icicles melting, dripping into a small river that flowed below us.

The next moment changed my life forever.

I looked up and saw that the path ahead was clear. The light from above sparkled and danced on the snow on either side of the dark brown earthen path. Up the hill, I could see that the strong, healthy trees protected the path and the green shade of the trees acted as a shield protecting the path from wind.

I realized my path was clear. Light surrounded and delighted me, protecting me.

As we took a few steps on the path and started up the hill, I realized my search for meaning ended. What I was looking for was God.

This quote deeply impacted my method of decision making early on in my journey of following the path of my heart:

> The way to choose happiness is to follow what is right and real and the truth for you. You can never be happy living someone else's dream. Live your own. And you will for sure know the meaning of happiness.
> —Oprah Winfrey

Do you feel trapped? Are you awake in your life? Are you afraid to choose your happiness?

So there you have it, an overview of my story. At thirty-one, my life plateaued. I walked around in the world thinking I was infertile. I felt ashamed, desperate, and angry. I looked happy to the world, but I was very sad. I judged myself using faulty beliefs formed in childhood. I felt disconnected in my marriage and hopeless about the future. I filled my home with stuff, trying to fill myself up. I blamed my husband for past opportunities lost. I tried to change him because I wanted to change my life. I over-drank. I overate. I over-shopped. I isolated myself. I cried a lot. I cried in my bathtub.

When I think back, this was definitely not a happy time. I will not share all of the personal details of the gradual breakdown of my marriage, as this is not the purpose of this book. However, today, several years later, I am so thankful for these experiences because they provide a measure of how far I have come since that time. I now know my strength. I now know my voice. And now I can share what I have learned.

I have helped hundreds of people create more meaningful careers. Many at one point or another lost hope in their strengths and skills, questioned their self-worth, or felt the immense pressure to just get a job and simply pay the rent. I can't tell you how many times, I have heard a client say, "I have sent out one hundred résumés and heard nothing back," or "I go to interviews and never get the job." And I can't tell you how many more times the answer to the question, "What do you really want?" is a defeated, "I don't know."

Fearful thoughts are paralyzing. Pondering the question, "What do I want to be when I grow up?" sounds like a luxurious dream state, as many people focus on the question, "How can I pay the rent?" However, it is by following what is really in your heart, recognizing and building your foundation on your divine strengths and qualities, that you not only pay the rent but thrive in the world. And this is where I start with all of my clients. For all of the people who enter my life, we always start here: "What do you love to do? What makes your heart sing? What is happening when you are joyful?"

And then it happens. Amid the fear and panic, I witness darkness part and be replaced with at first tentative excitement, followed by immense joy, hope, and clarity. If I wait long enough, people usually start by saying, "Well, what I really want to do is ... " Then people recall vividly a joyful moment along their journey, and this awareness and recognition of their dream bubbles to the surface, and they believe once again happiness is possible.

This is my passion: witnessing this rediscovery and clarity of self. It is like people are holding their dreams gently, like a fragile glass ball, and extending them carefully up toward the light and outward for others to see. It requires great courage to show others what is in your heart. But please believe me, it is possible to discover your dream and also pay the rent. If you are not convinced, please keep reading through this book. I truly hope you will be inspired to open your heart to the possibility.

When I am working with people, I always acknowledge this courage for sharing their experiences with me because when the dream surfaces, expansion occurs and their lives shift, however slightly, and others can feel this shift too. The affects of this shift is not always certain, and things will change.

Embrace your life exactly as it is now and focus on the goodness that exists, no matter how small because it is this goodness that grows and transforms your life!
—Kelly MacLellan, M.Sc.

Before this time, I focused and drowned in the thoughts consuming all of what I didn't have, just as the law of attraction states what you focus on expands. This is so true! So now that you have decided that enough is enough and are ready to choose your happiness, it will not only impact your relationships, your career, and your health but will also inspire other people, including your family and friends, to pursue authenticity in their lives!

In life, you are going to be introduced to day-to-day situations that will demand a response, so why not choose to respond mindfully and with intention? Make change—which is an inevitable force in life—work for you by knowing who you are and what you want! Spend the time and enjoy the journey, getting to know your inner voice and learn about want you really want.

There are no mistakes, no coincidences. All events are blessings given to us to learn from.

—Elisabeth Kubler-Ross

There are two mistakes one can make along the road to truth ... not going all the way, and not starting.

—Buddha, Hindu Prince Gautama Siddhartha,
founder of Buddhism, 563–483 BC

1. Identify What You Want to Change.

We are so fortunate to have so much information available to us about how to live our best lives. However, at times it can be overwhelming. Experts agree when we are faced with too many choices, it can prevent us from making a decision. And even when we do choose, we feel as though we missed out on another better opportunity. It can become difficult to choose what direction to go in when all of our options seem wonderful!

The same applies with information. There are many exciting developments in personal and spiritual development that we have access to via the Internet, but what is useful for us? I am sure you can identify spending hours reading blogs, scanning websites, and listening to podcasts and radio shows. There isn't enough time to absorb it all! How do you sort through all of the information, techniques, tools, and connections?

When you begin to strengthen your connection with yourself and really hear your voice, you will be guided to the resources that will help you along your way to self-discovery. When you have tapped into this flow, people and circumstances will begin to enter in your life, and opportunities will flow to you. You will think that this is just good luck, but really you are the one attracting these new events into your life.

Simply stated, when you connect with your inner voice, this means being connected to that place within you that is divine. This voice can be called your Higher Power or your soul. Your soul is energy of the spiritual world. Spiritually, our souls are all connected through a collective consciousness; therefore, what we do in our individual lives has an impact on the rest of the world. There is great opportunity to heal the world when we understand our spiritual connection with each other and also a great responsibility to humanity to contribute our very best. When we approach life from the soul level, we connect with this divine energy within us and align naturally with our higher purpose.

Think about it: where do you think our goals and dreams come from? Why don't we all have the exactly the same goal, dream, or purpose for our lives? Dreams are hints and messages signaling to us to follow our passion, our life purpose, and to pursue our potential. We can't push them away for long because they are always popping up here and there. You are unique. There is no one else in the world that is exactly like you with your gifts. The world needs you. You are perfect just as you are, and you have something very special to bring to the world and other people around you. The world is waiting for you to act on the messages in your heart!

Life is going to happen regardless. If we passively approach change, it can leave us feeling helpless, disappointed, stressed, and angry about situations in our lives. It makes sense, then, to assume a proactive and mindful approach to change, listen, and create what we want in our lives, embracing our divine gifts, talents, and purpose! But where do we start? We start with the truth.

Truth

We are all intuitive and have a sense about what is true or right for us. We all have had feelings about situations or people in our lives and received a signal that something just wasn't right. This uncomfortable feeling warns us to be aware of danger. When we go against or try to ignore our intuition, the result is the creation of unnecessary challenges in our lives. It is much harder and requires more energy to go against the natural flow of our lives, pushing and forcing things instead of flowing and moving with the circumstances presented to us.

In order to find our truth, we need to stop struggling and take a step back from what we are doing and listen. Listening and gaining awareness is real progress, but in order to harness change and follow our hearts, we need to not only get quiet enough to hear, but we also need to be honest with ourselves about what we find and accept ourselves exactly as we are.

We instinctually know what we need and what isn't working in our lives, but this usually happens at a subconscious level. Consciously, we might not be able to clearly name what we need or what the real problem is because admitting our faults and our deepest desires is not always easy. As I mentioned earlier, once we gain awareness, the truth becomes more difficult to suppress, and change enters the picture. Change represents both the unknown and also possibility. If you dread change, it leaves you feeling vulnerable and sometimes paralyzed. However, if you see change as representing new possibilities, it is exhilarating and wonderful! Therefore, we might keep the truth hidden in the subconscious because being aware of it means we will have to act on it.

Our truths, which are the same as saying our beliefs, are formed very early in life and are greatly influenced by our environment and the people around us during these formative years when we are too young to make intelligent, rational conclusions. Therefore, the early experiences we had are still very much alive in our lives today because they shape the way we look at the world! Consider that we are now adults and making decisions based on information stored in our subconscious when we were infants and children!

These "childlike" truths are at the root of our daily decision making; they shape our behaviors and affect the success of our lives. Because our truths are shaped so early in our lives, we have been making decisions and practicing the same behavior for many years. We also develop coping strategies early on in our development to protect ourselves, and because of this, we can be very creative in coping with weaknesses and disappointments in our lives. We may want something to change, but we find it difficult to modify our behavior and find excuses to dismiss our inability to change. It isn't until we gain self-awareness and believe in our worth that we can let go of old, faulty beliefs, be aligned with our truth, and finally receive happiness and peace.

We can all identify with a time when we weren't happy; we may have wanted a better job, more money, better relationships, and more energy. When we aren't happy, we sometimes do outrageous or desperate things, possibly hurting people or ourselves in the process. Our progress may halt because of fear, and we become depressed and begin using substances to buffer the pain. We may become angry and stressed out, avoiding the real issues, yelling, or being abusive to others.

Think about how you cope with difficulties. What do you do when faced with change? What usually happens as a result of this coping response? If we look back throughout our lives, we will likely recognize a pattern and see that the same issue and the way we cope continue over and over again. Take some notes, and capture any insights. Why do we subject ourselves to such drama and pain over and over again? Why don't we learn? Why would someone who is highly functional in some areas have chronic relationship, health, or money problems? Why do we continue with these behaviors? We do because these repeated behaviors are based on old untruths or faulty beliefs. Until we uncover and identify these untruths and intentionally create new truths, we will continue to repeat the same behaviors, with devastating, unwanted, or negative consequences in our lives.

I was functional in some areas of my life, but during those sad years in my life, my coping strategies were very poor. In order to cope with the pain of having a miscarriage, I regularly consumed large portions of food and wine to fill the void I was feeling. And when I wasn't eating or drinking, I was shopping! I filled my house with stuff! My spacious house was full. I was surrounded and wanted more, more, more! I had everything materially that I could ever want, yet I felt empty inside. I desperately searched for answers and meaning to help heal my heart. To illustrate my relentless quest for meaning, I once walked into a bookstore and asked the assistant if she could help me; I told her that *I needed something more in my life* and asked her if she could *help me find meaning.*

This memory makes me smile because I asked this poor woman, truly believing that she could direct me to a single place outside of myself where all the meaning that I yearned for resided. Even now, I can still see her face as it went blank. I can still feel the sad, desperate tears as they sprung to my eyes as we looked at each other uncomfortably. I was so sad. It was obvious that my pain was mounting and what I was doing to try to cope with my pain wasn't working.

Sometimes it is hard to admit that we want something new or different. We search, excuse, justify, or deny things just to keep our lives the same as possible. Admitting to wanting change can be very scary, so instead we tell ourselves, "It really isn't so bad" and keep pushing through life. This strategy consumes so much energy!

Often when we are pushing forcefully through life, we do not allow much space for self-reflection or examination. If we keep busy enough, we don't have time to deal with our emotions or any of these issues we are running from.

To give us a clue about what we might be avoiding, consider the following questions and see if anything triggers a response in you. To rephrase this, we are looking for the drama in your life. Think about your relationships, your career, and health and wellness areas in your life:

- How much time do you spend wanting something different than what you have right now?
- Have you said to yourself, "Enough is enough!" and vowed to change?
- Do you daydream about how good your life would be if you had what you wanted in your life?
- Are you dealing with the same thought, drama, or issue over and over again?

If You Still Don't Know Where the Drama Lies in Your Life, Can You Identify with This Scenario?

Imagine a time when you really wanted something, like to fall in love with a perfect mate, lose twenty pounds, move to a new house, or quit your job. When you have thought of something, think back to when you were coping with this issue. You talk to your friends about the issue. You complain about the issue. You lay in bed at night wishing that the issue was different. You wonder when things will change. You become tired and irritated about dealing with the same thing over and over again. No matter what you do, it still persists! What else can you do? You feel like you have tried everything! You feel ready to throw your hands up, surrendering! You feel hopeless and defeated; *it all just seems so big!* So you convince yourself it isn't an emergency and put it off for another day. You don't have the energy to deal with it right now. You wish that the issue would go away, and if it did, everything would be better.

What Is the Issue for You in Your Life?

Whatever the issue is in your life, it is a clue to what you really want to manifest. The yearning for the perfect mate, losing weight, finding a new house, and securing a better job all represent incongruence between what you have and what you want. However, sometimes what we think we want isn't always so; for example, sometimes we say we want a new job, but with some focused exploration, what we discover is a desire for more creativity. Before we can uncover the deeper issue, we first have to clarify what we want on the surface. Let's continue to examine what is going on.

How Do You Know When Something Isn't Working in Your Life?

ACTIVITY 1: *Free Thinking.* As I mentioned earlier in the introduction, to manage the information I am presenting here within this book, I have categorized life into three areas. If there are things you would like to change that do not necessarily fall within these categories, please write these down too.

These three categories—relationships, career, and health and wellness—will also serve you to focus the insights that are generated while completing the self-exploration exercises.

Without censoring your thinking, consider the following three categories, and write each word as a heading on a separate page in your notebook:

1. Relationships
2. Career
3. Health and Wellness

As you look at these headings, what initial thoughts spring to your mind?

Write or draw names, ideas, issues, goals, likes, dislikes—anything that you feel or think is related to each heading in your life. Write them down freely on each page. If we move on and you think of something new that relates to these areas, feel free to go back and capture these thoughts in your notebook.

Examine Your Beliefs

The beliefs we hold as adults are often developed as children and based on experiences using immature decision-making skills. Often our truths do not apply to our current reality or are even contrary at times to what we believe now to be true.

Have you ever blurted something out and then paused, realizing that you don't even agree with what you just said? For example, beliefs like, "You have to sacrifice to be happy" or "True love only happens once." When we are young, we accept others' uncensored versions of truth as our own truth, and then we judge the world from these faulty places in our thinking.

Words, phrases, stories, information, and all of the stuff from the past do not need to define who we are today, yet we tend to refer to them, restricting ourselves in our present lives, often subconsciously. It is time to let go of past beliefs that are no longer true or benefitting us!

What Is Your Story?

We have all had dramatic events in our lives; some of these have shaped and changed the direction our lives have taken. Throughout the sequence of dramas, we have assumed a role, usually the same role in each event to some varying degree of intensity. These roles can range from comedian, hero, victim, princess ... The roles we assume have a lot to do with where we fit in our family dynamics while growing up.

The subtleties of how our family dynamics impact us can be illustrated in the following example. Mother speaks at the dinner table composed of extended family members, filling in all of the latest news on her two children. "Oh, you know Amy; she works so hard, staying up late studying. You know she has straight As this term and is going to be a doctor some day. I am so proud of her! Oh yes, and Adam. Well, he is always playing games, being goofy with his friends. He keeps us all laughing around here. He's the social one." If these messages were heard frequently enough, Amy can be labeled as the hardworking, brainy type and Adam as the goof off joker. These roles will follow Adam and Amy through life and likely hold on to them even though they no longer fit!

> When I let go of what I am, I become what I might be.
>
> —Lao Tzu

Can you identify? Write your thoughts down now in your journal. Let's examine what is going on.

ACTIVITY 2: What is really true? In order to uncover the truth about our current reality, let's take a look back on your life and some of the main events that have shaped your current story of who you are as a person.

a) Turn your journal sideways, and draw a line across the page. This line represents your life until the present. For each decade, put a little tick on the line and then another tick to represent a main event. A main event is any event that you feel has impacted you either positively or negatively. Number the main events, and then beside each corresponding number, record in point form what each life event was and briefly how it impacted you.

To illustrate this exercise further: across your page, if you are forty years old, you will have four ticks with several events in between. In the first decade from age zero to age ten, you might have ticks that represent events such as winning a race, learning to play the piano, dealing with your parents' divorce, or being teased by a group of children at school.

In your next decade, from age eleven to age twenty, you might include your main events to be graduating from high school and getting a job or instead traveling through Europe or having your heart broken. Your next decade, from age twenty-one to age thirty, you might include gaining or losing weight, being hurt in an accident, losing friendships, learning a new skill, or falling in love. Your next decade, from age thirty-one to age forty, might include having children, taking up art, starting a new business, going on a personal development retreat, or suffering the loss of a loved one.

Whatever shape or direction your life story has taken up to this point, we are looking for some main events that have impacted your life perspective.

b) Review these events as a whole and also on their own, consider the following questions, and record your responses in your journal.

- What do these events have in common?
- Are there themes or beliefs that repeat themselves throughout your life?
- Do you share the same beliefs as your parents? Friends? Family?

- What were you told when you were young that you still hold onto as your truth?
- What story do you use to describe yourself to other people?
- Does this story really express who you are now and what you believe in?
- Does it feel like the right time to let this story go?
- When your parents speak about you and your siblings, how do they talk about you?
- Do they compare you with your siblings?
- What words are often associated with their description of you?
- Are these words, stories, and beliefs true to you today?

In addition to this exercise, feel free to explore your story further if you want to take more time by writing it out and how it has shaped your present beliefs and values. Go ahead!

Is There Something You Are Ignoring in Your Present Life?
Quiet your thinking, and consider that question. We are really good at suppressing things that are hurtful or seem out of our control, so be gentle and patient with yourself as you consider this question.

We say yes:

> I want to lose weight, but I will start on Monday.
> I want to stop drinking, but there is a great party this
>   weekend!
> I want a better relationship, but I will call them later.
> I want to stop smoking, but I will quit after this pack.
> I want to have a better sex life, but I have a headache.
> I want to get a new job, but I don't have time to do my
>   résumé.

All of these things we say we want and are going to do but never end up doing begin to change the way we view ourselves. Monday turns into Tuesday and then Tuesday into Wednesday—then, heck, the whole week is shot, so let's just try next Monday, and then week by week you procrastinate and give up entirely. You give up because you can't trust yourself to follow through, and you lose faith in yourself. Does this sound like you?

Even when you do follow through and you lose that five pounds or you quit for a week or a month—you feel good because you are doing it! But then something strange happens. We think privately, *I am doing so well ... I will have just one more doughnut, one more cigarette, one more drink, and/or one more shopping binge* and then you are back in it. The temptation leads you back through this pattern again and again.

How do you feel at the end of this? Out of control? Sad? Hopeless? Possibly, or maybe you have justified your self-defeating behavior. Everyone else is struggling, and I see that they have tried and they have failed, so why should I think it should be different for me? Your thinking turns into: *I really can't get what I want, so why even try anymore? I have tried so many times. Why should this time be different?*

Many times I have heard a client say something to the effect, "I think there is something wrong with me. Maybe I am just depressed or have Adult Attention Deficit and Hyperactivity Disorder." What these statements imply is, "This is so big for me. I have no control, and I can't do it." Sure, there is a possibility that these clients could be clinically depressed or have ADHD, but psychological labels, especially those self-diagnosed, have a way of becoming an escape route from taking personal responsibility. If accurately diagnosed and with the proper medical intervention if necessary, the next step is psychological counseling, which will teach a person techniques to exercise personal choice. Therefore, even if you have a diagnosed psychological condition, it always comes back to choosing your behavior.

The point is, you can change your behavior and attract more of what you want in your life if you really want to do some honest self-exploration. My question to you is *do you really want to get honest about what is holding you back?*

For a few months, my client had shared her desire to change her evening ritual to improve her quality of sleep. She was tired of drinking too much caffeine late at night, eating big dinners, and falling asleep to the late-night chatter on the television. Together we created a list of tasks to implement along with stating a clear benefit of implementing these tasks—quality sleep will improve her quality of living during the day. She followed through for one weekend and immediately fell back into her own routine.

When I approached her for an update, she reported she couldn't make the changes. I asked her, "Are you really ready for change?" She paused and stared at me almost like she didn't hear the question and then continued to share with me her suffering and all of the detrimental effects of living without proper sleep.

What would happen if you got what you wanted? What would change? Who do you think would be affected if you made these changes in your life? Is this fear of the unknown the real reason that is preventing real change from shifting your life toward the ideal? Are these fears based in reality? Write down any insights now in your journal. Let's examine what is going on.

Facing your fear is the only way to overcome it. I had to face the fact that I was afraid to get what I wanted. Once I shook off the fear,

I know this to be true: if you really want something, you will get it. And if you doubt and believe somewhere inside of you, "Sure, I would like to have that or go there, but I really can't," then you will be right and you won't get what you want.

Whether you think that you can, or that you can't, you are usually right.

—Henry Ford

ACTIVITY 3: *Clarifying the deeper issue.* So go back and consider the three main areas of your life again: relationships, career, and health and wellness, and consider and write your responses to these questions.

- Is there one thing that you always complain about when talking with other people?
- Is there a person in your life who annoys you? What is this person doing to you that is bothering you so much?
- Do other people give you advice and try to help you? What is it that they are saying to you? What do they want to help you with?
- Are you exactly the kind of man or woman you want to be?
- Who or what is to blame for you not being who you want to be?

Our environment is a reflection of how we feel and think about ourselves. The friends we keep and the conversations we have with other people as well as with ourselves create our life experience.

We have the power to choose and create a different experience. Admitting that your life isn't perfect and there are some things you want to change is not a sign of failure. You don't have to pretend anymore that everything is perfect in your current life. Sure, opening yourself up to wanting change can leave you feeling afraid and vulnerable at times, but it is not a sign of failure! Failure is when people choose to give up when they are aware that they are capable of more or a better way of living. Living in truth is to live in congruence with your deepest values and beliefs, growing toward your potential.

I ran into an old friend recently. She told me about her growing kids and about her job that she loved. I commented how full her life sounded and congratulated her how much love was in her life! Then she shared that she stays very busy because she and her husband separated the year before. She can't stop because she was afraid of stopping and what would surface. A few days later I saw her again from a distance rushing through the supermarket at full throttle, a pace that no one could keep up forever.

Make the Decision to Change
Admitting that you want something different in your life is a sign that your inner voice is getting stronger. When you allow that little light of possibility to grow, you begin to believe that the future really can be different. In order to clarify what you want, you need to risk falling apart. And if you fall apart, with a gentle approach, listen to your thoughts and the messages being sent from your body.

Keeping a fast pace is preventing your authentic voice from emerging. By allowing the light of possibility to grow and hoping for something different in your life, you are sending out a new message that says, "I believe in myself and am going to invest time and access resources and meet new people to help me live a life that is more ideal with what I want." By hoping for even a little bit of change, you are choosing to live a more authentic life that is more aligned with your beliefs and values. Wow—that is huge!

When you set out to change elements in your life, it is helpful to know how you measure success. How will you know when you have gotten what you asked for? In this next activity, I suggest that you explore your perception of success and failure. The questions might uncover reasons that your past attempts did not work out the way you planned and also shed light on your current commitment to lasting change.

ACTIVITY 4: *Explore your personal beliefs about failure and success.* Write your responses in your workbook and later journal on your responses.

- What do you think failure is?
- What do you think success is?
- What signifies success?
- What do you want to change in your life to make it more successful?
- Do you feel hopeful that you can create success in your life?
- How will these changes change your life?

Sure, there will be times when you want to sink back into ignorance where little in your life changes. But floating in the safe waters of a pond is much less exhilarating and rewarding than accepting the challenge of following your heart and jumping into the wild rapids!

You could float and wish you never started this change process, but eventually the pain of giving up and not attempting to follow your dream will return. Be gentle with yourself, and ease back into the process when you are ready. I will share techniques in a later chapter on how to get through those times of wanting to give up, but for now, take a moment to sit back and congratulate yourself for making it this far! You are doing great!

Activity 5: *Clarify what you want to change.* Review the following areas of your life—relationships, career, and health and wellness—and return to your list from Activity #1.

Identify what you would like to change in these categories by circling them or rewriting them on a new page in your notebook. Remember, if there are things that you would like to change that do not necessarily fall within these categories, please write these down too. By completing this exercise, you now have specific information about your life that you want to change.

Activity 6: *Setting an intention.* Now that you have clarified what you want to change in your life, it is important to set an intention for *how* you want to go about approaching change.

Consider that every company has a mission statement or vision for their organization. The mission statement might include key words or values such as compassion, honest, respectful, enthusiasm, passion, creativity, etc.

For the purpose of this exercise, setting an intention is synonymous with creating your plan ahead of time about how you want to approach achieving what you want. Make a decision about the kind of attitude you want to exude or are aiming for before you set off toward achieving your goals. Be proactive rather than reactive!

How do you want to "be" during this experience? Consider your values and things that you think are important. What do you pride yourself on? What have you tried to teach others about because you think they are important? What words resonate with you?

When you are faced with a roadblock, how do you hope you will react? Fearless, patient, calm—these are all possible answers to dealing with roadblocks, which will absolutely happen. Choose what feels right for you.

When you state a clear intention, it serves as a clear message to yourself and the universe for how you want to be during this growth process. It can also be a way to bring you back on track if you stray away from your intention.

Review all of the areas that you want to change from the previous exercise (Activity 5), and take a moment to think about your intention for your journey. Clearly set an intention stating: "I intend to ...

I encourage each of my clients to *enjoy* the process of self-discovery; however, you might be more comfortable saying, "I intend to embrace this change with an open heart." Another example of an intention might be, "I trust this process and have faith that all is well."

One of my beautiful, gifted clients named Grace entered life coaching with the intention to let go of relationships that no longer served her. She intended to create space for newness to enter. She yearned for magic. These intentions guided her through difficult decisions and situations she faced as she intuitively followed messages and signals from the universe and transformed her life and most recently fell in love with her beloved new partner.

Only you know what is right for you. Select an intention that feels right for you. Set this as your intention. Write it down. Keep it close, and refer to it often. Now you made the most important step the first one!

Happiness can only exist in acceptance.
—Denis de Rougamont

What the mind can conceive and believe it can achieve.

—Napoleon Hill

2. Create a Picture of Your Life Purpose

Now that you have admitted and identified what you would like to change, the next step is to get clear about what it is you really want. Through a series of activities, we will create a clear vision of what you want to manifest if you were living aligned with your life purpose. To aid in organization, we will categorize the images of your vision into the three main areas of your life: relationships, career, and health and wellness.

Whatever it is that you want in your ideal life, you must become the person who would attract all of these things. For example, if you were living your life purpose and highest potential and your perfect mate is interesting, cultured, and healthy, chances are that your perfect mate is looking for someone who shares these similar qualities and someone who can interact socially with him or her. So ask yourself, are you interesting, cultured, and healthy? Are you whatever quality it is that you want other people to be for you, in your ideal life?

ACTIVITY 1: *Imagine you living your ideal life.* Relax. Find a place that is quiet or inspiring. Open your notebook to a fresh page, and close your eyes and quiet your mind.

Imagine that your life is flowing perfectly, and everything is ideal; there is peace all around you. All you feel is harmony, and your body is soft and relaxed. Read and ask yourself each of the following questions, and then close your eyes again and let yourself travel to your ideal life. Imagine yourself now in your ideal life.

When you open your eyes in the morning, what does your bedroom look like?
What kind of house are you living in?
Where is your house?
When you look out of your windows, what do you see?
Who do you wake up with?

What activities are you doing during your leisure time?
Who are you spending time with?
What is happening in your relationships? Use key words.
How are the people in your life talking to and treating you?

What professional skills and personal qualities are you demonstrating while at work?
What responsibilities do you have?
What comes naturally to you?
What are you wearing to work every day?
What are you spending your money on?
What do you do after work?
What kind of books, newsletters, papers, and magazines do you read?

What does your body look like?
Run your hand over your ideal body. Feel your skin and different body parts. How would you describe your ideal body?
Spend as long as you want experiencing your ideal life. Enjoy this beautiful place and feeling!

ACTIVITY 2: *Create a vision board!*

I created my first vision board in early 2007 after watching and being inspired by the movie *The Secret*. I have uploaded a copy of it on my website for you to see at www.embraceyourlife.ca. My vision board was such an integral part of my life transition that I even brought it with me when I went to the Dominican Republic! It is very personal, and at first, I felt a little vulnerable sharing it with others in my work. However, after much thought, I decided to share it with the hope that it might inspire you to create one too and that you will experience its powerful impact in your life as well.

I would set up my vision board in front of me while I worked, or it would accompany me when I would take long candlelit baths. And if I was in my bedroom reading, then I would lean it against a wall in my bedroom.

Having constant, clear, and vivid reminders of my ideal world guided my behavior toward what I really wanted in my life. Whenever doubt surfaced, I chose in favor of my pictures. I am a very visual and hands-on person, so this method of the vision board really worked for me. You may be different, but that isn't a reason not to do this exercise. You can capture your ideal world by creating your own video with audio and watch or listen to it every day. You can even simply write down everything you want and then record yourself describing your dreams. There is even vision board software available if you want to create a computerized version of the vision board.

Basic steps to creating your own vision board:

- Collect a variety of magazines from a variety of sources.
- Gather art tools: glue, scissors, and a piece of Bristol board.

- Put on some music and relax, breathe, and open your mind and your heart.
- Avoid judging and criticizing or limiting your imagination, and begin flipping through magazines, tearing out anything that stands out for you.
- Tear out pictures of things, people, ideas, words—*anything* you want in your ideal life or that represents a feeling of what you want to create in your life.
- Organize the pictures, piling them into the three main areas—relationships, career, and health and wellness—and another pile for other various and special pictures or phrases.
- Arrange the pictures creatively, cutting them if necessary, and secure them onto the Bristol board using the glue.
- Place the vision board in a place that you see regularly.
- Each day, for as little or as long as you want, look at the pictures on your vision board and close your eyes. Using your imagination, transport yourself into your ideal life, and use your senses to experience these pictures.

To illustrate the power of the vision board, for example, look at the bottom right corner of my vision board. There is a woman who is writing at her desk in front of a laptop computer; there are books piled all around her. Her desk is in front of enormous windows that overlook the ocean. Nearly every day, I would close my eyes and imagine myself as this woman. I would imagine sitting at my desk in this office, that I was holding her pen and writing a letter to my best friend describing the beautiful view from the window. Not even a year later, I was this woman, and that was my office! It was incredible! And I am not exaggerating the degree of accuracy!

Since this time, I have created three more vision boards, because as you manifest your dreams, you will have more dreams and then even more dreams. You will continue to grow and will want to bring these new pictures into your life! Keep your vision boards as a reminder of your journey and accomplishments.

ACTIVITY 3: *Share your vision.*

a) Find a supportive friend or partner to assist you in this exercise.

The purpose of this exercise is to bring your partner with you when you travel into your ideal life. By sharing your ideal life with someone else, it is reinforcing the reality of its existence and the possibility of your ideal picture to manifest. I think that supporting someone at this level, holding an intention for someone, and sharing in his or her experience as his or her vision partner is the main element of this visualization technique being successful. One reason is that if your partner can see it too, then you will believe that it actually may be possible! And if your vision partner knows what you really want, then you will be more accountable to your ideal vision. It will be harder to talk yourself out of!

If you cannot find someone you trust to help you with this activity, imagine that I am sitting across the table from you and describe to me in great detail the pictures you see when you are living your ideal life. Another idea is for you write your thoughts and then record your voice. When you do this, you are stating your intentions more firmly than if you simply wrote them out and reviewed them to yourself.

b) Engage your senses.

Using the description of your ideal life and the pictures that were generated from Activity 1 of this section, choose one specific element of your ideal picture and imagine having it. For example, imagine driving down the highway in your new car or standing on the tallest building sipping champagne or sitting on a rock overlooking the ocean while watching the sun set with the most beautiful partner holding you securely. Whatever it is, be there. Next, imagine a person enters the scene and takes a fifteen-second video of you experiencing this situation in its perfection. Now imagine watching that fifteen-second video and ask yourself:

- How does it feel?
- How does it smell?
- How does it look?
- How does it taste?
- How does it sound?

Now that your senses are engaged, let's apply this concept to each of the three main areas in your life: relationships, career, and health and wellness. You may decide that you would like to focus on one area rather than all three areas in your life. If that is the case, please skip to that list of questions within this section. Please take your time with these activities. When I work with a client and lead them through these exercises, we usually take approximately one and a half hours per life category.

Relationship: Continue working with your partner or alone writing out your responses.

- Describe your ideal partner. (Ask the sense questions above, feel, smell, look, taste, sound.)
- What is it about this person that is most ideal?
- Describe your relationship with each other.
- What happens in your relationship that makes it ideal?
- How does it feel to have the ideal relationship?
- How are you as a partner?

- What kind of qualities do you contribute to the relationship?
- What qualities does your ideal partner enjoy in you?
- Describe your closest friendship.
- What qualities do you value in a friendship?
- If the world is a perfect place, how do people relate with one another?
- What makes you a good friend? Daughter? Brother?

Complete these sentences, and write out your answers:

In my ideal life, my relationships with my family and friends are ...
My family and friends describe me as ...
In order to have good relationships with family and friends, it is important to ...
In my ideal life, my romantic partner would describe me as ...

Summary:

In my ideal life, my relationships can be described as ...

Career: It is common to hear statistics reporting that there are many people who are unhappy or unchallenged in their jobs. Would you describe yourself as one of these people? Do you feel capable of more responsibility in your current job or company? Or are you ready to explore a new career entirely?

Continue working with your partner or alone writing out your responses.

- When you close your eyes and dream about the perfect way to spend your time during the day, what are you doing?
- Imagine that you are completely exhilarated and focused at work. What are you doing?

- When people speak about you, what are the qualities they admire about you?
- What is unique about you?
- How do you get to work?
- What do you enjoy spending your money on?
- Imagine having all of the material things you want now. Describe using your senses what it is like having them.
- When you feel completely competent, proud, and rewarded at work, what are you doing? What skills are you using?
- In your ideal career, how much money are you making?

Complete these sentences, and write out your answers:

When I was a child, I was known by my friends to always ...
When we would play, I always ...
I used to dream of being a ...
When my parents would talk about me and my siblings, they always said that I was the ... one.
When I get ready to go to work on Monday morning, I feel ...
If a problem arises at work, I feel ...
When I leave my job to go home, I feel ...
When I talk about my job, I usually say ...

Summary:

In my ideal life, my career can be described as ...

Health and Wellness: Continue working with your partner or alone writing out your responses.

- When I am in perfect health, what do I look like? How much do I weigh?

- Imagine touching your legs and feet and rubbing your arms and any other part of your body. Describe how your ideal body feels.
- Look at yourself in a mirror. Look into your eyes. What do you see?
- If you could wear the perfect outfit when you are in perfect health, what would you wear when you are feeling happy? Sexy? Professional? Imagine yourself in these three outfits.
- Tell me about your hair. How would you ideally wear your hair? What color, length, style?
- Imagine getting ready for a sexy date with your partner or new friend, and look at yourself in the mirror. How do you feel? Excited? Nervous? Giddy with anticipation?
- How are you looking after your health each day to maintain your perfect ideal weight?

~~~~~~~~~~~~~~~~~~~~

- What are your sleeping patterns? Imagine waking up after a good night's sleep. How do you feel? What time do you get up? What time do you go to bed?
- What professional care do you have in your life to support your healthy lifestyle?
- A dermatologist, a psychologist, a chiropractor, a massage therapist ... Formulate the perfect group to help you look after your health and wellness needs.
- Imagine yourself scheduling these appointments and sitting in the waiting room. Imagine talking with them about your health. How do you feel?
- Describe your ideal routine.
- What do you do before breakfast? Yoga? Read? Journal? Walk? Water the garden?

- What do you eat for breakfast?
- What hobbies and personal development activities are you participating in during your leisure time?
- How are you involved in the community?
- How would you describe your relationship with nature and animals?
- How do you describe your beliefs pertaining to spirituality or religion?
- In your ideal world, what important values drive your behavior?

Complete these sentences, and write out your answers:

My ideal body can be described as ...
When I am in perfect health, I am having more ...
My personal ideal style is ...
My perfect day is when I spend my time doing ...
My deepest beliefs and values are ...
I participate in my community by ...

Summary:

In my ideal life, my health and wellness can be described as ...

ACTIVITY 4: *State your life purpose.*

You might think, **What?** *I can't decide what my life purpose is already!*

Well, you really don't have to. It is highly likely that your life purpose statement will continue to develop and evolve as you practice new behaviors and apply what you are learning. But what we can do is try to bring it together into a clear statement that will serve to guide your behavior throughout the program.

Step 1: Review your three summary statements above, and write them here below:

- In my ideal life, my relationships can be described as ...

- In my ideal life, my career can be described as ...

- In my ideal life, my health and wellness can be described as ...

Step 2: Circle two key words from each summary statement and then ponder the question:

What do you feel (in your heart) you are here to do on Earth?

Write down your initial response to this question, and then write out the six key words from your ideal life.

Now blend together your ideas from the question and use the six key words to create one or two concise statements about your life purpose. Write your statement(s) here:

My life purpose is to:

_____

_____

Please note, I made a conscious decision to not include examples of other people's life purpose statements here to avoid influencing your discovery process. I chose this to reinforce the fact that no life purpose statement is better than someone else's. A life purpose statement could be elaborate, heroic, altruistic, or even stated in three words. Each one is unique—just like you!

Congratulations!

I know that was a long exercise! However, understanding your ideal life at a sensual level is pivotal and therefore one of the most important steps in moving you toward living aligned with your life purpose. By completing these activities, you have clarified your picture of your ideal life as it relates to relationships, career, and health and wellness. *And* you have generated clarity around your life purpose!

Take a moment to relish this moment! You are doing it one step at a time! I hope that you are feeling excited and can feel the momentum building. By the end of this chapter, I trust that you have taken down detailed notes and created a vision board capturing your ideal life. It is time to go to the next very exciting step in this process—to begin aligning with your vision and life purpose!

> At the center of your being you have the answer; you know who you are and you know what you want.
>
> —Lao Tzu

If we all did the things we are capable of doing we would literally astound ourselves.

—Thomas Alva Edison

3. Begin to Live your Life Purpose.

We now have a clear picture of our ideal life and some insight into our life purpose. We can see and feel how we want our life to be ideally and are ready to make it happen!

Activity 1: Create a Sacred Space
In coaching, one of the first items of discussion is creating a quiet space for reflection, meditation, and creation. This space does not have to be an entire room; it could be a corner of your bedroom or family room. One of my clients has even turned a large closet into her private space for meditation and prayer. Wherever it is located in the house, fill it with beautiful, inspirational items and music that envelop and uplift you. Create an altar (mine is created from two suede boxes stacked upon each other) where you can place meaningful items and reminders of the things that uplift your spirit.

Paint the space the color you want. Hang inspirational art to motivate you and energize your passion. Fill it with comfortable pillows, encouraging you to stretch your body and mind to the possibilities. When you get seated comfortably, review the summary statements collected in Activity 3(b), "In my ideal life my life can be explained as ..." and your detailed notes about your relationships, career, and health and wellness areas.

Grab your vision board, and have it beside or in front of you. Use your senses now. Look at the photos, feel, smell, hear, touch, taste what it feels to have these images as your reality. Do you feel good? Get in touch with how feeling good feels.

The more we identify with our vision and feel good, the faster we will see the change take place in our lives. Our behaviors will change, and we will let go of things easier because they simply do not fit with our ideal life; things that previously bothered us and other pesky issues seem to drop away. What used to drain us disappears because it is simply not aligned with our ideal pictures.

I also want to take this opportunity to remind you to continue or begin the essential practices of the Follow Your Heart Program: a regular practice of yoga, meditation, nature walks, daily journal writing, and sharing this experience with an accountability partner, friend, or coach. These essential practices add structure to your daily routine that will support your healthy growth and self-awareness. Now that you have also created a quiet space to retreat to in your home, I encourage you to visit your sacred space every day and reflect on the day's events and the choices you made. As you go through this self-awareness process, record and review your notes regularly and journal on these following questions:

- How does it feel to take the steps toward creating your ideal life?
- Do you like the person you are becoming as you make different choices?
- What changes are you starting to see take place now that you have identified what you want in your life and are nurturing your relationship with your soul?

57

Your work is to discover your world and then with all your heart give yourself to it.

—Buddha

You Are Powerful! You Have Choices!

In late August 2007, I was stretched out on a Dominican beach, gazing at the sky with the turquoise ocean extending out in front of me. I laid there soaking in the heat and pondering my journey and the adventure I was about to embark upon. My journal was tilted on my lap, and I was feeling a bit giddy. *How did I get here? I am so happy! I feel free! How did this happen?*

How did this happen?

Only months earlier, before I arrived to soak in the rays of the Caribbean sun, I crumbled under all of the pressure from the battling thoughts in my mind about what I should do and where I should go, I had the harsh realization, *I don't know myself anymore.*

I felt lost. I surrendered and prayed for what seemed like hours. A soothing feeling comforted me, and I heard the words, whispered softly, "Kelly, only you know what to do. Just follow your heart." Immediately, I knew and was empowered!

For days afterward, I was quiet and focused internally and created a picture of what I really wanted for myself in my ideal life and what the ideal me really looked like, what I sounded like, and what made me happy. Then I visualized living and being this way every day. I spent my time exercising, doing yoga, writing, and breathing consciously. I knew what I wanted. It was very clear. In my mind, I already even had it!

From there everything moved quickly, and my inner voice became very clear and strong. It was time to act on my intuition. Nothing else mattered. I acted on the belief that only I am responsible to create the life I want. I was very tired of complaining, so I stopped. My inner voice whispered the words trust and faith, so I did both.

In order to align with my ideal life, as I shared earlier, my husband and I separated. We sold our house, and I donated most of my possessions. I intended to live a simpler life, and instantly, I felt lighter and freer. This decision felt right. My body reflected my new state of mind and let go of the pain and heaviness, and I lost twenty-five pounds. My outside matched my inside. A new intention formed: to create a life that was passionate and interesting.

Aligned with my new vision and intention to live with passion and interest, I also decided to leave my job and pursue my dream of writing and coaching. While I have been blessed and loved my decade-long career, I wanted to take some time off to explore parts of my personality that I didn't have the space or time for before. I wanted to volunteer and learn a new culture and language. So I did.

My family thought I had lost my mind!

I faced a lot of concerned criticism, questions and fear but it was my clarity and trust in my inner voice that lead me through their rational arguments. I created clear boundaries about the support I needed.

There were lots of reasons why I shouldn't do what I was doing, I knew this because I had thought, considered and feared all of them. But no reason was as rational as the feeling I felt when I trusted and followed my heart. I felt great! And that "feeling good" feeling was the cue I followed down the path through this pivotal time in my journey.

Within 6 months of deciding to listen and follow my heart, I was laying there on the beach ready to begin the next chapter of my life in the Dominican Republic! And only a few weeks later, I was riding on the back of a motorcycle to an elementary school at the top of a mountain in the sunny Caribbean! Something I would never have imagined for myself! Every day was an adventure. I arrived at school each day by motorcycle and would jump off into the welcoming hugs of beautiful, loving little children. It was an incredible experience!

One of my first mornings teaching at the school, I stood at the blackboard and looked through the open windows at the cocoa trees that cascaded into the deep valley. I marveled at the glorious shades of green and clean air. I took a deep breath and became aware of the experience of bliss.

I felt bliss in this moment looking at my students with the green tropical background in the simple concrete building with loving energy circling all around me. My body was tingly, my smile was peaceful, I was laughing, and time stopped! Pure bliss!

We started singing the ABCs, and as we sang, tears rolled down my face. I was listening. I was listening to my heart, and it led me to the most beautiful place in the world! I was getting closer to discovering my life purpose. Joy and bliss continued to guide me closer. I faithfully followed.

> And all things you ask in prayer, believing, you will receive.
> —Matthew 21:12

When my full-time volunteer placement finished, I then asked the universe for one year to write and share my passion, all with a view of the ocean. I also asked to fall in love with a beautiful, kind-spirited man who loved to cook and dance.

And guess what happened? Everything I asked and set an intention for came true!

Most of these words in this book were written from my apartment with a view of the ocean that I shared with my new partner, who passionately loves to cook and dance! He also closely resembles the man I imagined months before when I captured him on my vision board!

Along with the image of my handsome new man, my vision board also had words and phrases: *inspire, share your passion,* and *choose happiness, bliss, and passion.* These also manifested in several ways in my life.

By choosing in favor of these words, my life purpose emerged. People began e-mailing me and asking me for advice, wanting to get unstuck from their own life situations. I started sharing my passion, and my business, now called Embrace Your Life Coaching, formed. My mission to inspire others to live authentically was formed.

I discovered my life purpose to inspire and empower others through my writing and teaching to believe in themselves and follow their hearts! All of this beauty entered my life because I listened, trusted, and followed my own heart!

Change happens moment to moment; therefore, each choice you make during each day is important in moving you toward your dream. Today could be the day you get the big breakthrough, or it could be the day that you are learning a valuable skill that you will utilize later on in your journey. You never know for sure what is going to happen. And usually when it all plays out, things happen even better than you could have planned for yourself!

One of my favorite things to say is, "I wonder what is going to happen today!" When I share my sense of wonder with others, my heart lightens and I feel a bit giddy, especially when I see that they too begin to feel the excitement. When something happens throughout the day that isn't what I would have chosen to happen, I view it as God's plan unfolding perfectly, and I look beyond to what is coming next because the plan is usually much better than we can expect. It is not denial of what is happening; it is acceptance that whatever is happening is meant to teach me and prepare me for what is yet to come.

Dreams are possible when you stay focused and believe that today is an important day in the unfolding of the master plan! Stay focused by asking yourself this question throughout the day:

**Are my choices moving me closer or
further away from what I want?**

Use this question when facing a decision or when you find yourself getting worked up about something. Again the question is: are my choices moving me closer or further away from what I want?

I recently facilitated a creative expression and personal growth program, and midway through it I asked each of the participants to name three things that had changed in their lives since starting the workshop. One woman quickly answered, "Nothing." I asked her if this was true. She hesitantly said yes again; it was true that nothing had changed in her life. Gently, one of the members touched her arm and said, "Sue, didn't you say earlier that you just went to a one-day art class and also signed up for an upcoming women's retreat?" Sue smiled and agreed that was true. I encouraged her to think of other things she might be overlooking. She said that she and her husband recently attended a wedding and her relative took one of the first photos of them in a very long time smiling and laughing together as a couple. She said it was a wonderful moment! Wonderful! Our group supported her, and she shared another development. She gave into the invitation and picked up a hockey stick and went out and played with the kids! She got down and dirty and loved it! We all watched Sue's demeanor change; she looked radiant. Things were indeed changing!

So, before you answer too quickly, using the old, familiar ways of communicating, make sure you are telling the truth. Sue was actually making choices moving her closer to what she wanted, which was fantastic, but she didn't communicate the experiences accurately. However, when she became aware of her healthy choices, she was elated.

It is very helpful to look to your body for clues of congruence with what you are saying to what you are feeling. We are human and sometimes fall out of flow with life. If I find myself in a rotten mood or facing something I perceive to be miserable, I look at my emotions and the messages my body is sending me, and I know that I am not following my heart. I catch myself mid thought and say to myself, "You are choosing this perspective! You are choosing to look at things negatively." Then I quietly or sometimes abruptly place my hand over my heart, listening for the beat to return to my center, and ask, "What good is there in this situation? Is there any room for a new perspective? What can I learn here?" I relax as my heart and thoughts slow down.

Activity 1: *Analyze your choices.* Think of a day when everything seemed to go wrong. You know, the kind of day when it is raining, you forget your umbrella, your pants get wet, you need to go to the gas station, which makes you late for work, etc. Oh yes, and then you come home after being stuck in traffic and have a fight with your partner over what to have for dinner! That kind of day ... If we are experiencing a difficult period in our lives in our relationships, careers, or health and wellness areas, we tend to focus on what the difficulty is, and they begin to multiply. Remember what the Law of Attraction states: what we focus on expands.

Go through that one day, think about those challenges, and examine the choices you made that contributed to this challenge. By seeing how your choices impact your situation, you will develop objectivity and clarity about your ability to choose and therefore create a different life by choosing different behaviors.

Ask yourself:

- What relationship choices did I make today? Did my choices move me closer or further away from my ideal picture?
- What career choices did I make today? Take note that making no choice is in itself a choice.
- What health and wellness choices did I make today? Did my choices bring me closer or further away from my ideal picture?

When you become aware that you have a choice in your reactions to situations, this awareness will help improve your situation immensely. You will feel more empowered to handle situations, taking more time to think before responding, listening to what it is you really want, and then aligning your behavior with your ideal life.

It hurts your situation when you feel and act like a victim. Victims tend to think that things are always *happening* to them and that they are *powerless*. Choosing this victim behavior will move you further away from your ideal picture. So if you are beginning to feel beaten up by the world—and it does happen to most of us from time to time—remember to always ask yourself the question: are my choices moving me closer or further away from what I want?

As you practice asking yourself this question I learned when studying Choice Theory by William Glasser, it will become more natural to choose behaviors that make you feel good and are moving you forward, the positive behaviors that are aligned with your ideal picture. Eventually, you will instinctually look after yourself and do only what makes you feel good, and you will get very familiar with how goodness feels in your body.

> The only person whose behavior we can control is our own.
>
> —Dr. William Glasser

Let Your Heart Guide You

I repeat throughout this book to "follow your heart" for emphasis because truly listening to my deepest desires and trusting myself, especially when I faced my biggest fears, worked! Even when things seem grim, there is always hope! The way to get out of your "grim" situation is to realize that the search for meaning and answers is not an external search but rather an internal one. To begin this journey inward, you need to get out of your way and let your heart guide you. What does that mean? It means acting from your heart and not from your head.

> Conscience takes you where others want you to go. Integrity takes you where your soul wants you to go.
>
> —Gary Zukav

I want to clarify at this point the difference between love and lust and the physical differences between receiving either one. When you lust after something, such as a new lover, a new car, or a powerful position, and selfishly follow your urges and desires and do whatever you can in order to obtain these items, you will likely be left feeling empty even if you do achieve these things. Being lustful and pursuing immediate gratification is based on the ego's need to fill itself up with stuff, words, titles, and falsities. The physical feeling experienced when you follow your lust is an adrenaline rush, false pride, fear of being "found out," and hollowness. Lust leaves you feeling unsettled, hung over, and lost.

When you follow your heart, you trust your deeper intuitive self. You show love to yourself and to others. The physical reaction when following your heart is like a glowing white light beaming in all directions from you but concentrated from your chest—your heart. Time disappears and all is radiant. You feel peace and joy.

Our egos usually talk us out of something because of fear of the unknown, but our hearts always lead us to what we truly desire. When you follow your heart and receive its desires, you will feel good—really good! Therefore, trust what feels good in your heart and use this feeling as guidance; this "feeling good" is aligned with our hearts.

Activity 2: *Guided meditation to open our hearts.* Read the following paragraphs several times, becoming very familiar with the words, or record them by reading them aloud to yourself and play them back to yourself.

Get into a comfortable position, either sitting or laying down. Sit or lie down quietly and close your eyes. Breathe in and out, feeling your breath spread into your lungs and out through your nose. Feel your chest expand and deflate.

Put your hand over heart and feel for its rhythm. Listen very closely, and feel your heart's beating with your hand. Feel its strength. Feel its warmth. Feel its pulse. Imagine a small white light shimmering in your heart's center. Imagine this white warm light spreading through your body from your heart. Your body glows with this pulsing white light. You are calm.

With your hand remaining on your heart, a smile spreads across your mouth. You are amazed at your heart's perfection and effortless beating.

Quietly, listen for any messages that are shared with you. Be quiet and wait. Listen to your breath. Listen to your heart.

When you are ready, move your hands to your side and open your eyes softly. Record your experience in your journal.

To follow your heart means that you will live mindfully, aware, in the moment. You will be tuned into what is happening within you and around you, aware of how you are feeling. If you are ever out of awareness, bring your hand to your heart, and listen for its messages. You can do this simple exercise in the middle of a meeting at work, to calm yourself during an argument, or even to celebrate an achievement!

Complete these activities with a partner or alone, recording your answers in your notebook.

ACTIVITY 3: *Feel good and choose happiness!* Perfect moments are when you are truly present in the moment, when nothing is missing and nothing could be added to make the moment better. You feel bliss. It is selfless; you don't need to do or be anything different. You feel slightly removed, non-attached; you just witness it. The purpose of this exercise is to really identify those times when you are the most happy and blissful and to be aware of how your body feels when you are happy.

- Can you think of a perfect moment—a moment when time stopped and all was blissful? Write it down and then close your eyes again and remember the way your body felt when you were in this moment.
- When you have at least five happy and peaceful moments, open your eyes and look over your list. When reviewing your list, see if there is any relationship between them. I looked at my perfect moments, and from the similarities, I developed a happy list. Here it is:

> My happy list is:
> 1. Sun/beach
> 2. Yoga/meditation
> 3. Teaching/learning/writing
> 4. Dancing/music
> 5. Nature

Let's extract some happier, feel-good information from your life. Ask yourself the following questions and record your reaction in your journal.

- What makes me feel good? What fills me up?
- When am I the most energetic?
- When am I happiest?
- How are my relationships and daily experiences affected when I am happy?

Record any insights you have and write down anything else that you can think of that makes you happy. Often after completing the exercise, people find that they have experienced more happy moments than they thought! Delicious meals, special moments with children or animals, and the thrill of overcoming a challenge are all things that people begin to add to their happy lists.

I remember one woman at a retreat I co-facilitated sharing her joy about taking a bubbling apple crisp out of the oven and how the sweet smell spread through the kitchen as she lifted the first portion onto her plate. She oozed joy when she shared this memory! We all agreed that these simple experiences are within our reach and experienced every day.

How do you feel so far? Record these ideas or insights in your journal. Next open up your day timer and consider how you can incorporate some of these happy items into your schedule over the next day, week, month, and year.

When you begin to collect items for your happy list, try not to eliminate items because they occurred on your wedding day or the day your child was born or the day you hit your first home run. These special events cannot be recreated. If you can, try to extract the feeling of what was happening in that special moment. Remember, it isn't the event you are looking to recreate but the feeling you felt being with the people at the event. Maybe it is time to call and rekindle some friendships or simply just connect with a loved one or maybe picking up a favorite activity again. It can be as simple as that!

My client Ann loved curling up in her beanbag chair under the windows that overlooked her large treed property. There she would read for hours upon hours. She daydreamed, listened to inspirational music, and indulged herself in hours of rest and self-care. She passionately shared how much she loved her dogs and their daily long walks together and how peaceful she felt when she re-entered the house.

Commit to creating happy moments in your life by deliberately setting an intention and making an appointment with yourself to do it! Your day timer may have entries for going to the gym, going to an art class, booking a girls weekend at a bed and breakfast, calling your best friend from school, planning your garden, cooking your favorite recipe, volunteering, etc.

Aligning your behavior with your ideal life happens one choice at a time, one moment at a time. Getting in touch with what feels good in the present moment helps motivate us to make healthy choices each day. Knowing what makes us happy helps us gain clarity and choose more of these happy activities to add into our routines. Review your "happy list" and your life purpose statement regularly and choose more activities to add to your day that are on your list and aligned with your life purpose!

To emphasize how easy this is to apply, you can see that I am happiest when I am dancing and listening to music. So with this in mind, one day I sat down and downloaded my favorite music into my iPod and keep it with me wherever I go. I can energize myself or soothe myself all with the music. I also listen to music when I cook and my husband and I dance in the kitchen. I don't wait for a night out to dance. I break out my moves every day! I look for ways to inspire and empower myself so I may radiate that energy out into the world through my interactions.

By recognizing the positive effects of making mindful choices, we become motivated to choose happiness and to feel good! And *choosing happiness* and *feeling good* are behaviors that are aligned with our ideal life! Great work!

> Embrace your uniqueness. Time is much too short to be living someone else's life.
>
> —Kobi Yamada

Courage is the power to let go of the familiar.

                        —Raymond Lindquist

4. Protect Your Ideal Picture

As you align with your ideal picture and begin to practice using your happy list and choose in favor of honoring your life purpose, people will begin to notice. People will say, "Hey, what's up? What is going on with you? You're acting differently. Why are you so happy?" These responses can evoke some uncomfortable and new emotional reactions.

It is normal to want to feel accepted to avoid judgment and criticism. Change can be very challenging to navigate, especially if you feel the people closest to you are not as supportive as you hoped they would be. Look to your mood, as it will reflect how you are handling the change. If you are feeling negative and grumpy, chances are your choices are not aligned with your ideal life, but not to worry—what you are doing is new, and there is a tool to restore your direction and regain a joyful state. But first, how do you handle people interrogating you when you are in no mood for their opinions?

Be Prepared
If you are feeling negative, grumpy, vulnerable, teary, emotional, or sensitive, avoid being impulsive or defensive when you respond to others. Choose your words carefully. Be delicate, even vague. Protect yourself and your ideal picture. If you find that you are continually being drawn into uncomfortable conversations, decide

what you are going to say before you are faced with these situations and only share with people the information you want them to have and no more. You do not need to explain your behaviors to others. You are responsible only to yourself!

To help illustrate this point, for example, transitioning into parenthood is challenging. New mothers and fathers have fears and questions. Simultaneously, they also have superb and wonderful moments during the first week following their baby's birth. They often are eager to share their excitement and joy, as well as the panic and difficulties associated with this big life change. Think about how many times you hear someone giving advice or criticizing the choices of these new parents after they open up and share their experience. There are many people ready to tell you what you should and shouldn't do and why this or that isn't a good idea. I have witnessed new mothers deflate and lose all confidence after being told they should try another way of handling a situation with their new baby. The new mothers weren't asking for help or advice but rather a person to simply listen to their experience.

Whether you are a new parent, changing a job, losing weight, or contemplating divorce, choose who you are going to share your news and story with. Not everyone knows how to listen. Know what you need from another person before you openly share with him or her. You may need to be direct and ask people simply to listen if that is what you need. Also, carefully select who you open up with; choose people who tend to be good listeners and people who openly share with you in a respectful manner.

A young woman contacted me recently sharing she was in conflict about her recent life situation. She was a college student in her late teens and was three months pregnant. I could see how being pregnant at a young age and not being married would be a cause for concern, but then I thought, *This is my interpretation of the situation and might not be hers,* so instead I carefully asked her how she felt about expecting a baby. She emphatically exclaimed and bubbled over with happiness! I responded with sincere congratulations about her happy news.

The young woman indicated the conflict was she wanted to quit school and stay at home and prepare for her new baby but felt everyone had an opinion about what she should do. Many of the people she confided in did not necessarily listen to what she wanted or to what the real situation was that she struggled with. She felt isolated with this situation and judged. If I had not first asked her how she felt about her pregnancy, my initial judgment would most definitely have been detrimental in helping her deal with her conflict.

If you are ever approached to be a listener, avoid judging the situation and gather more information first. And if you share with others, be aware that people usually will assess the situation based on their own personal experience, which will often have nothing to do with you.

What was my advice to this young woman who was engaged to be married and have a baby in six months? "Follow your heart; you know what is right for you." She got teary and agreed all she wanted was to "create a home for my family." She followed her intuition. I spoke with her recently, and she is a new mother and is very happy.

However, there may be times when you do not approach others to help you with your situation—you approach them to celebrate your situation! There are times in your journey when you are so excited about the positive changes in your life. You are overjoyed and want to share, share, share! Again, I offer a word of caution, even during these good times. Remember to protect your ideal picture. Have you ever shared exciting news only to have the other person point out something you may have overlooked, immediately dampening the joy? Ouch!

Have you ever run home or called your best friend, shrieking excitedly, *"I got the job! I got the job!"* And then he or she asks you tons of questions: What time do you start? What is the salary? Are you sure that is a good company for you? I heard that that industry has been hit hard, be careful ...

As discussed earlier, people are very happy to share their opinions and offer suggestions, so if there is any area of doubt in your head about whether you can actually achieve your ideal picture, be very selective of who you share it with. Talking about your dream with someone who doesn't understand or respect your vision will find and say exactly what it takes to break open that small, subtle doubt you have and turn it into a massive, gaping hole full of doubt and fear. You will go from feeling elated to feeling squished and won't know why! So be wary, trust yourself, and protect your picture!

> Every time I've done something that doesn't feel right, it's ended up not being right.
>
> —Mario Cuomo

ACTIVITY 1: *Practice filling yourself up with joy!* When something wonderful happens to you, keep your good news to yourself for one day, and if that seems like an eternity, just try it for one hour and gradually hold it in for longer. Instead of calling your best friend with news about your new job or new relationship, hold it in! Dance, celebrate—express yourself, alone! This is a fantastic exercise for getting to know how your body feels when you feel good. Feel the excitement inside. You are making a conscious decision to celebrate it all on your own! You did it! Then, when you are ready, share it with someone you trust and celebrate more!

When it was time to replace the family vehicle, Jenny and her husband started researching and test driving cars together. They narrowed it down to several possibilities and left the final decision to Jenny because she would be driving it more frequently. Jenny took a few afternoons off of work to drive cars and narrowed the list down to two.

Both cars were suitable for the family's activities. The first car was efficient and available immediately. But the other car made Jenny feel really happy. There was something special about the design, the shape, and the sleekness of the interior. It too was efficient, but it was not available immediately and not in the color she wanted. In her mind, she imagined herself driving a blue car.

Feeling the pressure of needing to purchase a vehicle, she felt buying the blue car was selfish when it seemed superficial and inconvenient for the family, but something inside of her said, "No, I am going to listen to what I want." So she did. She ordered the car that made her happy in blue. But what happened next surprised Jenny and the salesman. Her car just became available in the next city and it was in the color she wanted—blue! When Jenny's car arrived the next day, she went out for a long drive and celebrated her success! She shared with me afterward how good it felt to listen to that voice that told her to do what she wanted. She felt really good.

Going out into the world and being different, thinking different, being happy even can rub people's feathers. Some will say, "Who does she think she is? Or why is he so happy? What is wrong with him? People can't really be that happy!" And the list goes on ... unhappy people love to bring other people down! They are vibrationally drawn together. So this is where trusting yourself comes in.

Handling the Transition

There are stories of people who have lost significant amounts of weight and because of their drastic weight loss and change in lifestyle, these changes seriously impacted their relationships. Some of these people lost contact with friends and partners, or oppositely, they impacted positively and inspired each other, creating something wonderful together!

It is important not to push your new lifestyle choices on others. When you change your behavior, it impacts your primary relationships. Friends and family may become inspired by your commitment to self-growth and jump on board, or they may feel completely put off, hurt, and rejected. They may have different ideal pictures and start moving in other directions or aren't interested in examining their behavior and are simply happy with the way things are. You cannot force people to change or make them want something different. You are beginning to understand more clearly now that just as you are on your personal journey, so is everyone else. Just like everyone else's way isn't right for you, your way is not the right way for everyone else.

One of my longtime clients created a vision board and kept it hidden away from her family and any visitors to her home. She told me she felt vulnerable. In her words, she said she was not powerful enough yet to stand up for what she really wanted. She instinctually knew she had to approach change slowly if the entire family was going to be supportive of her dreams. I saw her struggle continue for months until she had a breakthrough after a conversation with her husband, and slowly she started to share more and more about what she wanted to do with her life.

If you and your family are experiencing problems communicating during this transitional period, suggest to your loved one that you seek professional counseling together. Professional help will assist you both to effectively adjust to changes in your relationship. When confronted with possibly losing friends and family, you may be tempted to quit and forgo your ideal picture in order to salvage your relationships. You might think what you want isn't worth losing your relationships for. Get quiet, listen to your internal voice, and trust that you are following your heart and doing what is best for you. Ask yourself, *Does this feel good?* Whatever your response is, acknowledge it. It is okay to adjust your ideal picture if that is truly what you want. But quitting with the intention to save your relationship will only breed resentment. So go ahead and change the picture! It is okay. And if you are following your truth and are honest with your intentions, then the relationships that are best for you will endure.

Developing Our Sense of Worth
ACTIVITY 2: Value yourself. Know your worth! A common belief that prevents us from living fully is that we are not good enough. There is a part of us that thinks if we had more or were better or different somehow our lives would be complete. This is a faulty belief. We are already enough. Making the shift away from this faulty belief and cementing a new belief about valuing ourselves takes practice. It is immensely important to believe that you are worth it and that you deserve to have what you want.

In a quiet place, write the words across a blank page, *"I am worth it and I deserve to have what I want."* How do you feel writing this statement? Do you believe it?

If believing this statement is difficult for you, use it as an affirmation throughout the day. Write it repeatedly in your journal, and place it somewhere visible for you to be reminded of its strong message. When you feel doubt or hesitation, repeat the affirmation to yourself.

I am worth it, and I deserve to have what I want.

Watch as your strength, power, and trust build within you. When you begin to feel and see these improvements within you, recognize the connection between these new feelings of empowerment and changes in your thinking. Affirmations work, but you have to use them.

If you continue to find this affirmation challenging to believe, try inserting the name of your child or grandchild, your best friend, or your favorite family member. Do you think they are worth it? Of course you do.

When you make positive changes that are aligned with your ideal life, you are actually impacting the people you love by inspiring them to make positive decisions. You are inspiring change and teaching them how to honor, respect, and discover themselves just as you are doing in your own life. So if you aren't yet at the place to make the changes for yourself, then do it for them! The more you learn about loving and respecting yourself, you are automatically teaching them simply by trying to heal yourself!

I have a beautiful, kind friend who recently took one of my workshops. For as long as I can remember, Emma has been a creative, patient, quiet soul who supported her friends lovingly and loyally. She decided to take the creativity workshop to shake her life up a bit and get out of a rut she was in. When she was cleaning in her bedroom, she found an old box that had some torn-out magazine pictures about dreams she wanted to manifest for herself. They were pictures of design, events, and inspirational quotes. As she sorted through all of these images that she collected over ten years before, she realized that these images still soared in her heart.

During the workshop, Emma participated in her regular manner. She was observant, supportive, and gentle, and she took the homework assignments seriously. She wrote every morning and explored her community, trying new things. She gathered all of these old images and more and created the most unique and colorful vision board. She proudly shared her books—yes books—of images and declared her passion and vision to the group: to be an event coordinator, specifically a wedding planner. She sketched out her future home office and began removing items in her home, clearing the space for the new to enter. She researched the appropriate training courses and bookmarked them in her computer. However, a few things blocked Emma from embracing this vision. She feared her husband's response and wanted to be taken seriously. She balked, and her writing stopped.

When we get close to our dreams, the fear sometimes intensifies, "protecting" us. Knowing this coping strategy of protection, as a group we shared our self-sabotaging experiences, and from this discussion, Emma felt encouraged to share her vision and career plan with her husband.

She returned to the group the following week, light, even buoyant, and shared her recent development. She felt such a sense of relief and renewed connection with her husband, and her heart was full. She also shared that her children were excited and joined in supporting her vision and helped her clear out the space for her new office! She jumped in with two feet and registered for the training courses; it flowed effortlessly, and she was supported by her family.

Ultimately, you are responsible only for yourself. You are the only person who can choose happiness; in other words, only you can make you happy. As Emma's experience illustrates, the dreams we have in our hearts exist and remain there waiting to be nurtured for years and years. Our dreams are divine gifts meant to be used to fulfill our life purpose. Each of us is unique, with our own talents and skills. When we embrace these gifts and recognize that we are meant to share them with the world, the only action we need to take is to step aside, get out of our own way, and let the process flourish.

> Begin to see yourself as a soul with a body rather than a body with a soul.
>
> —Wayne Dyer

If we block ourselves from sharing our gifts because of fear of what others will think, we dim our light in the world. Embrace this belief: it is not your job to persuade other people to your side or to your way of thinking. Let go of trying to do the right thing or what you think other people want from you. Gather your courage, be real, and follow your own truth, and trust the dreams in your own heart. The changes you make in your life might not make any sense to other people, and they may openly disagree and question why you want what you want but that really doesn't matter. When you believe in your worth and share your uniqueness, it gives other people permission and teaches them to follow their own hearts and create more of what they want in their lives too. I believe that Emma's children are learning valuable life lessons about self-worth and authenticity from their beautiful mother as they dream and plan together as a family and see their mother step forward boldly and create what is in her heart.

> What we see depends mainly on what we look for.
>
> —John Lubbock

Focus on What You Want
Vision boarding is a powerful tool for manifesting what you want in your life. It is very easy to let your mind wander to places of defeat, powerlessness, and fear. When we become intentional

about our thoughts, our behavior follows. Just as negative thinking can compound and lead you, spiraling toward feelings of depression. Positive thinking can compound and generate powerful feelings of hope and possibility. Creating a vision board reinforces what we want to attract into our lives and keeps our thoughts focused intentionally.

My vision boards hang in front of my workstation. Most of what I imagined for my ideal life is here in my present reality, and the rest is clearly on its way. When I am visualizing and experiencing my ideal pictures on my vision board, I feel joy spread throughout my body. I am really happy and excited about what I have!

In the middle right area of my first vision board, I organized pictures of love and romantic relationships. These last years have brought me so much more in this area than I could have asked for! But the most remarkable change in my life was related to fertility. I didn't know how I would become a mother because I thought I was infertile.

When I was selecting images for my vision board in early 2007, I chose a beautiful picture from a magazine of a new mother holding her newborn baby. The mother and baby are naked. You can't see their faces, but the way they hold each other is magical. The mother is tenderly holding the baby to her body instinctually. I wanted this image to manifest very deeply in my reality. But I didn't know how it could happen—until it did. In my journal in February 2009, I wrote:

> For so many years, I walked around in the world thinking that I was infertile. I spent a lot of time thinking and feeling damaged, incomplete, and unworthy, and as a result of these thoughts, I carried large loads of pain. I felt this way until I decided that enough was enough, and I set out on my journey to follow my heart.

For nearly two years, my work with Dominican children taught me so many lessons about trusting others (including myself), loving others (including myself), and giving selflessly (toward myself). My heart has overflowed as a result. There have been times when I questioned myself. Why am I here living in the Dominican Republic? Why do I continue? What is my future?

My partner and I regularly attended a gorgeous church built in 1510 in our neighborhood in Santo Domingo. I continued to write in my journal:

One Sunday morning a few months ago, I prayed. I said, "Thank you, God, for bringing me to a place of peace in my journey. I finally understand, God, why I am here. If I am not meant to have my own children, I have at least found these beautiful children that I can mother."

I continued to pray with tears running down my face. "If this is why I am here in the Dominican Republic, then this is my destiny. I accept this," I sobbed. "Thank you, because these children are so special and share with me so much love!"

The next morning, I found out that I was pregnant! My dreams came true after four years!

I want to be clear and emphasize that my story is not to say that the only happy ending for a woman facing infertility is to have her own biological baby. I write this because the happy ending is about finding peace and surrendering. I learned about accepting myself. I learned about letting go of my questions of "how." I learned about having faith and recognizing that God has a plan and is preparing us for something special, even if we might not see exactly what it is or how it will come to us.

Whatever it is that you want, believe that it is possible. Change is inevitable, so why not choose to embrace the change and create your ideal life? Dream big! Put those pictures on your vision board, the ones that seem wild, unattainable, and impossible! These pictures really can come true and likely will be even better than you imagined!

ACTIVITY 3: *Visualize!* Recognizing that we have talked several times already about visualization, I include "Visualize!" as an activity to emphasize the importance of visualization as a tool in creating an authentic life.

To get through hard times when you are feeling hopelessness, review your pictures of your ideal life regularly. Get in front of your vision board, and immerse yourself in your ideal life at least once a day. Read through the exercises you completed early on in the Follow Your Heart program. Concentrate on getting focused on what you want. Experience the pictures on your vision board, or listen to the recording you made for yourself via audio. These pictures will transport you to your ideal life and restore clarity and confidence in yourself and remind you why you are making the decisions you are right now.

I knew that my decisions affected many people I loved, and I knew it was impossible to avoid this fact. I didn't want to hurt anyone, so I created the intention to be thoughtful, respectful, and supportive as my loved ones adapted to my news. For hours, I would listen to people's emotional responses, and I would sometimes quietly and sometimes angrily explain my viewpoint until I realized that these interactions actually distracted and drained me from pursuing what I wanted. Then it occurred to me that wanting to support other people is likely what got me into trouble and away from listening and following my heart in the first place. I was so concerned about not hurting people that I was choosing to look after others and not myself.

So I realized that I needed to stop responding to what other people wanted or what I thought they wanted, which I actually learned to mean two different things most of the time. Even when I heard positive feedback and excited praise about my decisions, I rarely responded because I knew that whatever they were responding to in my story had more to do with them than me. I tuned in to myself, my vision board, and focused on what I wanted and let all of that powerful energy drive my daily choices.

When you are making a change in your life, whether it is big or small, people receive this new information and attach value to it. When a person responds positively or negatively, this often has little to do with you but rather with his or her value system. Whatever information people received and what that information triggered in them is based on their personal experience. So even if their response is positive, although it may feel good to be accepted, their response has little to do with you.

A few years ago, I was working with an intelligent young woman as her coach. She had just been accepted into a prestigious graduate school and was unsure if she wanted to accept her seat in the program. She had been working abroad in a growing company and felt compelled to continue as her role in the organization was beginning to take off. However, the issue was that she felt pressure from her parents to attend school. Her parents worried that she would get distracted with life and never return to school, and she didn't want to disappoint them. She had only a few months to decide what direction to take.

We worked together to clarify her goals, and then I led her through visualization exercises. She described to me seeing herself walking down the streets of New York. She told me what she was wearing, where she was going, what she heard as she walked, and how it all felt to her. She transported me to her picture; it was so clear! Throughout these exercises, school did not even appear on the radar, so she knew what she wanted to do. She told her parents her decision to defer graduate studies and felt grounded in her decision. Eventually her parents accepted the decision and continued to support her. Not even six months later, she e-mailed me to tell me that while she was walking down the street, she looked up at the skyscrapers and realized that this picture came true exactly as she imagined it! We were thrilled! Now, almost two years later, she has been accepted again into graduate studies and knows that the time is right.

There is a way to stop all of this endless, mindless responding to other people's reactions and that is to trust yourself and make sure that your voice is the loudest voice you hear. Let that voice, *your voice,* guide you in the right direction!

Decide to Make Yourself Happy
In times of doubt or fear, I would close my eyes and immerse myself in the pictures, feeling good and excited about my ideal life. I would consciously choose activities, people, behavior, and thoughts that were aligned with what made me feel good.

When I would hear people questioning my decisions, I would say to them that I heard them and thanked them for their concern, but ultimately this was what I believed was going to make me happy.

For me, this step of trusting myself was a very intimate process. I turned inward often because I identified that my main problem, the one that got me to this place, was that I was living someone else's dream, someone else's expectations for my life. I did what I thought I was supposed to do. I made other people happy by being good and did what I thought they wanted me to do. I chose things that were safe because I was afraid of failing or being judged for being over the top or different. It was easier just to please people and conform.

It was now time to trust myself! In order to do that, *I had to get quiet.* During this time, I used a mantra and several positive affirmations. Mantra is a Sanskrit word for something used to help you focus your thinking.

ACTIVITY 4: *Recite your mantra regularly.* Review the following affirmations, and select one that resonates with you—or create your own. Write it out, become comfortable with it, memorize it, and use it throughout the day to restore calmness, compassion, and awareness to your behavior.

> I am only responsible to myself.
> I am exactly where I am meant to be.
> I choose behaviors that reflect my deepest values.
> I am gentle with myself.
> I am beautiful.
> I receive God's blessings and love.
> I live in truth.
> I love.
> I accept God's plan.

And the one I use nearly every day still to this point in my life is by Charles Haanel: "I am whole, perfect, strong, powerful, loving, harmonious, and happy."

ACTIVITY 5: *Be grateful.* Embrace all of what is going well in your life! Feeling grateful and recording your experience of gratitude will focus your awareness on all of the wonderful things that already fill your life. If we are too focused on the future, we lose sight of all of the goodness that already exists. When you feel grateful, you are in the present moment and interacting with the world from your heart. Watch how being grateful works in your life, and record the changes in your journal!

> When you are grateful fear disappears and abundance appears.
>
> —Anthony Robbins

Begin a gratitude list, and write on this topic of gratitude regularly in your journal. Each day, write three to five things that you are grateful for in your present life in complete sentences. For example, if you are writing in the morning as I normally do, you may write:

I am grateful for the restful sleep and my cozy bed. I am grateful that my best friend called me last night; I feel loved and cared for. I am grateful for this steamy coffee and nourishing breakfast; I feel fortunate.

You will notice the change in your behavior as you begin to look for things during the day that you are grateful for just so you can record them later on!

Overcoming Fear

Throughout this journey, you likely experienced moments of panic, became consumed with intense fear, and heard the voices of doubt and criticism boom in your mind! However, even during these uncomfortable dark periods, look closely at the center of all of this chaos and noise. There is a calming glow and presence.

This calming glow is your intuition, your inner voice, and your heart. It says to you, "You know that you are capable of great strength. You are powerful and wise and you are in this situation for a reason. Breathe. Everything will be as it is meant to be. You are safe."

Trust that you are exactly where you are meant to be. Trust that all of your decisions have led you to this moment. In this moment, in this place, with these people, there is something here that you need to learn. You cannot rush through this process. The lessons will always find you.

And in knowing that you are exactly where you are meant to be, know that you can never go back; you can only go forward. You are beginning to see what you are capable of. You have heard your true voice and are understanding now that living out of alignment will create more pain in your life because you know now who you are. It isn't always easy, but be gentle with yourself and others.

Activity 6: *Measure your progress.* Since beginning the Follow Your Heart program, you have faced your fears and opened your heart to infinite possibilities. Initially, you picked up this book because you had an issue that was troubling you. Remember back to the day when you first walked into the bookstore or if you purchased this as an eBook, think back to when you began searching through the book titles. Remember when you first opened this book and began to read. What was going on in your life in that moment?

Let's look back even further. Think of a time when you were at your very lowest—a time when you felt like your world was going to end: the day you lost your job, the moment you lost all of your money at the casino, or even after a nasty argument with your spouse.

If someone entered this scene and took video for fifteen seconds, how would that video capture you?

See yourself in this video. What do you look like? How can you show compassion for yourself now knowing all that you do now? Do you love that part of yourself? Even when you are at you are at your very lowest, see that you deserve love even then.

A New Door Opens

This process can be very painful, and you may feel completely alone and abandoned by people you thought would be there in your life at times. But remember, when one door closes, another opens. Yes, another cliché, but it is true! Pay attention to new people, situations, and things that enter into your life now that you are making changes. You are sending out a different message, sending out a different vibration to the world; you are opening up! When you are open to accepting new experiences that feel good, they will lead you closer to your ideal life.

It was during the first few delicate months of my transition that a beautiful, supportive friendship emerged. We gelled immediately, and within months, a small group of people entered our lives, and in many ways we became a family. This love and support lifted me up when I was afraid, challenged and opened me up to new possibilities, and celebrated with me. I was able to explore new facets of my personality that were emerging in a safe place. The timing was impeccable! I truly believe that God gives you exactly what you need!

> People come into your life for a reason, a season, or a lifetime. When you figure out which it is, you know exactly what to do.
>
> —Author Unknown

My intention when I share my story with you is to comfort, inspire, inform, create hope, and dilute anger or whatever else it is that you can take from it to help you navigate change. Each journey is different. That is why it is essential to follow your own heart and voice. When you trust that the answers lie within you, you do not need to feel threatened by other people. There is no need to compete. You can give and receive love and avoid being swayed by other people's input because you are following your own heart and trusting your own direction. You have made good choices so far to get you to this point. You are proving you are capable of great things!

There is not enough darkness in all the world to put out the light of even one small candle.

—Robert Alden

Life is not about finding yourself. Life is about creating yourself.

—Source unknown

5. Celebrate the Moment

Before we move into the information presented within this chapter, let's review our progress:

- You have identified the areas you want to change. You understand the benefits of embracing change and have made a commitment to yourself to begin the process.

- You have created clear pictures of what you want to manifest in your life. You know what you want and now have a variety of techniques to utilize throughout the creation process. Your life purpose statement is becoming clearer.

- You are beginning to live the life you love by choosing behaviors that are consistent with your dreams and your life purpose. You have created a structured routine inspiring daily introspection and practicing self-care aligned with your divine life purpose.

- You have learned to trust your intuition and protect your picture from the judgments and opinions of other people.

You have done a lot of work to get to this point. Congratulations! It is time to celebrate and receive the gifts being sent to you!

ACTIVITY 1: *Look for what is working!* Grab your journal and review your initial notes, specifically your intention and pictures of your ideal life. Look at what has changed since you began this process! There is no set guideline on the length of this self-discovery process, as it will be different for each person.

I started working with a woman named Julie who was pretty frustrated about a situation at home. She had wanted to make several changes around her house for the longest time, but her husband didn't want to spend the money. After thirty years of living in her home, she wanted new flooring and a dining room set. She shopped around, looking for what she wanted in her budget, but felt defeated and hopeless because every time she tried to approach her husband about making the purchases, he resisted.

Julie created a vision board. She began writing every morning and imagining that she already had the floor and furniture she desired. She told her husband what she wanted and didn't push the subject any further. She knew exactly what she wanted and where she could buy it. She returned to the flooring store that she had visited several times before but always seemed to miss the service consultant, but this time was different. The consultant was there, and together they reviewed all of the options and even found the flooring on sale! Julie arranged for a consultation for a company to quote the job to install flooring. She presented the information to her husband, and he said yes! Julie was elated! Her old carpet was ripped out and replaced with beautiful dark wood flooring. Her husband admired the flooring and thanked Julie for encouraging him to be open to the change.

Not wanting to push her luck, she decided to avoid broaching the subject of the furniture with her husband. However, not even two weeks later, when they were out on a drive she was stunned when her husband said, "Let's pull in here to this furniture store and see what they have in the way of dining room sets." Julie tentatively said yes, and together they walked in the store, found the perfect set, again on sale, and purchased it on the spot! *This is really working!* Julie thought.

Julie changed her approach. She got clear about what she wanted and focused on that and got different results. She attracted what she wanted effortlessly rather than forcefully.

So what is working for you? Review the main areas in your life and identify at least one way of how things have changed. It is very common to overlook events, dismissing them as luck or coincidences. Considering Julie's experience, when she went to look at flooring before she was clear, the service consultant was never available, but when she was ready, the consultant was there and the flooring was on sale! This was not a coincidence.

I urge you to avoid minimizing your progress and include even the slightest change that is aligned with your ideal life. It is important to recognize all of the success, as this is evidence for how the universe is acting in your life. The ability to receive success is a critical new skill to develop that will attract more success to you. I encourage you to list all of the successes!

Relationships:

Since choosing my ideal life, I have seen the following changes in my relationships ...

Career:

Since choosing my ideal life, I have seen the following changes in my career ...

Health and Wellness:

Since choosing my ideal life, I have seen the following changes in my health and wellness ...

Celebrate! You are doing it. Congratulations!

Honor and Respect Yourself!
Throughout this change process, you have made the decision to change the things in your life that you are not happy about. You have declared your intention and made daily choices, some that were very difficult. All of this action required great courage! You are letting go of fear and past ineffective behaviors. You are choosing to believe in yourself, and while at times you have been challenged, you have persevered! This is your time to shine! You really deserve to take a moment to relax, look around, and be proud for what you have started!

- Are you still practicing *savoring the success alone* before sharing it with others?
- What have you learned about *celebrating your success alone* first?
- What fills you up or brings you joy? How can you incorporate this joyful activity into your celebration?
- How can your celebration be aligned with pictures in your ideal life?

When celebrating, a lot of people think of indulging in excess, like food, alcohol, or buying material possessions. Have fun; enjoy what your heart desires. If your heart leads you toward the luxury of good food, drink, travel, and possessions, embrace it!

However, I encourage you to be wary of excessive indulgence, as the rush associated with these indulgent activities is often short lived and may even create guilt and disappointment, especially if you reward yourself with an inappropriately large piece of cake or smoking a few cigars after you set the intention to care for your body. Remember, the celebration should continue the good feeling, not destroy it! Eat a piece of chocolate cake; just don't eat the whole cake! Whenever you begin to behave unconsciously, you are not acting from your intention, and you will fall out of the flow with the moment.

When we understand at a heart level our divine worth and wholeness, material things are fleeting experiences. By not attaching ourselves to material possessions, we can enjoy them and experience life fully with joy because we don't try to own things; instead we enjoy them while they are in our lives. So celebrate your success mindfully and joyfully!

> Abundance is not something we acquire. It is something we tune into.
>
> —Wayne Dyer

ACTIVITY 2: *Plan to celebrate!* Think of a way to celebrate your success that is an experience and is aligned with your ideal life. Choose something that will benefit you, as well as other people.

Consider your ideal world and the kind of person you are when you are in your ideal world. If you have an ideal picture of being creative, join a creative group or class or pursue a hobby in art. If, in your ideal life, you are a community-oriented and compassionate person, then volunteer your time. If you are a cultured person, visit a new place or join an activity or group to meet new people.

If you have an ideal picture of entertaining and connecting with friends, explore your interest of the love good food and drink and visit a vineyard and take a gourmet cooking course. Then invite your friends over for a cocktail party! If you love to travel, plan your next holiday or even better, book it! Embrace your life, and trust the flow you are experiencing. Share your excitement and joy with the world! The point is to do something that you have always wanted to do and explore this new interest and watch it grow. Check the newspaper in your area for community events and workshops and go for it!

You never lose by loving. You always lose by holding back.
—Barbara De Angelis

Celebrate and Elevate with Music!
ACTIVITY 3: *Get your groove on!* Consider previous times in your life when you were happy and had moments of bliss. What music were you listening to at the time? Did you dance happily? Were you ever so excited about hearing a song when it was played that you were transported back to that happy event?

I remember the music that was playing on the radio the first time I was driving alone when I was a teenager and feeling invincible. It was fast and carefree! I also remember the music that I would dance to in my house, car and wherever else I felt the urge to dance to when I started this process. The music I was attracted to during this time was sexy, fun, and international. I let the music guide me, and my heart opened and my body fell into the flow!

Listen to your body—ask it what kind of music it wants to dance to in that moment. Spend some quiet time centering, choose the music, and then focus your energy on the part of your body that wants to move. Turn off the television and instead turn on the stereo and tune into some music that elevates your mood. Enjoy the feeling of the vibration in your body! Let the rhythm take control, as the phrase says, and stretch, move, and dance. Celebrate!

Celebrate by Toasting to Your Success!

Consider the changes you are seeing in your life now since starting this process. Think of all of the changes in your relationships, career, and health and wellness that you are seeing and take a moment to honor yourself. Think of these changes as being worthy of being acknowledged at a public event with a group of people.

At most celebrations, someone gives a speech or toast honoring the event with special words, quotes, and advice. If you choose to celebrate by gathering your friends and family together, consider giving a speech honoring your courage for setting out on this journey. This gesture reinforces your original intention to embrace change and also sends the message to the universe that you are practicing self care and are ready for more gifts to flow into your life.

An example of a toast would be: "Thank you for gathering here today. I am grateful for all of us being together. As you know I have made changes in my life recently and have felt lighter and more joyful as a result. The journey has not been easy, but with my loving friends and family, I feel supported. I wish each of you love, peace, and joy! Thank you!"

If you don't have a chance to publicly toast yourself and those you love, a way to honor yourself during your journey is to mail yourself a greeting card and post it on your vanity so you see it regularly.

It was not a coincidence that I continued to receive the message, "Follow your heart." After I shared with others how this phrase "follow your heart" made such an impact with me, I was regularly given gifts with this phrase on it from friends that ranged from an angel coin, a journal, and a bookmark. But it was when I was wandering through a store and saw a greeting card that said, "Follow your heart" on a day that I felt like giving up, I purchased it for myself. I went home and wrote an encouraging, loving message to myself. I addressed and stamped it and mailed it to myself. A few days later, I received the card, opened it up, and have kept it beside my bed ever since as a reminder of my intention to follow my heart and inspire others to follow theirs.

Celebrating your success and mindfully selecting methods aligned with your ideal life will result in increased awareness of the joy that is already present in your life. Your good feelings will generate more good feelings and attract more of what you want. Celebrate the fact that you are aligned with your ideal life!

Let us not look back in anger nor forward in fear but around us in awareness.

—Leland Val Van De Wall

The real act of discovery is not in finding new lands, but in seeing with new eyes.

—Marcel Proust

6. Realign with Your Life Purpose!

As you look back and see how far you've come, I trust that you feel good about your progress as you practice all of the techniques you have learned up to this point. You feel confident and self-aware. You have made recognizable changes in your behavior and routines. Yet lately, you are noticing something happening—people, situations, or things are triggering you to question yourself. They pop up unexpectedly or gently or violently, knocking you over the head intensely, demanding answers to the following questions:

- *Do you really think you can do this?*
- *Do you really believe that you deserve this new life?*
- *You are getting so much attention. Who do you think you are?*
- *You can't make this last.*

Don't Self-Destruct!
When old negative thinking arises, so do old coping patterns. Common coping mechanisms like excessive drinking, overeating, smoking, gambling, compulsive shopping, over-exercising, and watching endless amounts of television are all distractions from reality, and they are harmful ways of dealing with doubt and fear associated with adapting to change. Choosing these behaviors will move you further away from your ideal life.

When you are stressed or angry, try this simple technique to restore self-awareness.

- Observe your body for its response by doing a quick body scan from your toes to your head and feel the feeling of the rush of adrenaline running through your body.
- Try to quiet your mind by taking a deep breath and focus on how it sounds and moves in and out of your body.
- Sit quietly observing the change in your thought patterns and the rate of your heartbeat.
- Where does the intensity sit in your body? What does this intense urge want? And then listen for the answer.

Is there an intense desire to go out drinking, grab the nearest bag of chips, gossip, sit on the couch watching TV blankly, or go power shopping for hours upon hours? However you escape, numb, or tune out, it will work by lessening the intensity of the pain, but it will move you away from your ideal picture and you will get stuck in a rut.

Please be sure to understand what I am saying here. I am not saying don't drink, eat junk food, watch TV, go shopping, etc. Have fun, and do what feels good for you! I am simply saying if you are using these activities to avoid facing an issue in your life, continuing this behavior won't move you forward to where you want to go. Consider this quote:

> Insanity: doing the same thing over and over again and expecting different results.
> —Albert Einstein

Knowing your old patterns of coping and being honest with yourself is the first step in breaking the pattern. Stop the insanity! Watch for the old coping mechanisms as they arise during moments of stress, doubt, and fear. Get really familiar with the way they sound when you say them and the feeling in your body when you are saying them. These patterns may be disguised as ways to "celebrate," so watch for them in your casual conversations, like:

- Let's go for a drink!
- I will just have one more piece of cake.
- It is only $20 ... (Although you don't have $20 to gamble)
- I deserve that coat. I need to have it!

When you hear yourself using these phrases, say aloud or silently but directly, "I see you. I hear you. I know what you are here to do. You are here to distract me from my feelings, and I don't accept you as my truth." And then let the moment pass, taking a deep, cleansing breath afterward.

Try not to beat yourself up if you occasionally use these coping strategies to help modify your perception of reality. These strategies used to work for you, albeit temporarily, but they did work, and what you have to recognize now is that you don't need these old patterns anymore! You don't need to escape anymore! You have new behaviors that you have tested out and that work more efficiently!

You are evolving, and the authentic you is emerging and expressing itself in the world. Every moment you speak and share from your heart, you are releasing old patterns and learning new ways of living. This is *exciting*! So why escape from it? Let's learn how to embrace your life!

ACTIVITY 1: *Analyze your coping strategies.* Ask yourself these following questions, and record your answers in your journal.

- What coping strategies have you used in the past to deal with stress and anxiety?
- How did these strategies work for you in managing your stress?
- Did these coping mechanisms move you closer or further away from your ideal pictures in your ideal life?
- What new, effective coping strategies have you learned since starting this process?
- Why is it important to know your old coping strategies and develop new ones aligned with your ideal life?

Great work! I hope that you discovered a new level of awareness about your behavior. Let's continue to dig deeper.

ACTIVITY 2: *This too shall pass!* We have all experienced challenging times. Maybe we lost someone or were deeply hurt somehow. Think back to a time when you felt hurt or sad. How long ago was that? When you were going through that experience and feeling those feelings, it may have felt that every day was an excruciating day. But now notice that after two years, five years, and ten years, the pain is not as intense and as frequent. It passed.

Open your mind to this truth and understand that whatever the situation is that is triggering the response in you to cope, know that this feeling and situation will pass. Avoid acting impulsively, and sit with yourself quietly, getting in touch with the stress response in your body, and begin to focus on the rhythm of your breath.

After locating the pain and stress in your body, ask yourself, *How do I feel?* And then wait and listen. Get in touch with this present moment by using all of your senses. In this exercise, we are calming ourselves by creating distance and quietness in the space between our thoughts. I included my answers as an example; notice that

I use short, identifying words to describe my experience of the present.

Learn to calm yourself. Begin by gently closing your eyes.

- *What do you hear?* Birds, music, ocean, cars, voices, horns, hammer, birds, baby cry
- *What do you smell?* Ocean, sweat, heat, vanilla perfume
- *What can you taste?* Describe the feeling in your mouth.
- *What is your body touching?* Keyboard, heat from the computer, back against the chair, feet touching the ground, I can feel a slight breeze touching my skin.

Now open your eyes.

- *What do you see?* Computer, the clouds, earphones, palm trees, fan, TV, cell phone, wires, glass, mouse, paper, CDs, vision board

Now take two slow breaths. Repeat your favorite affirmation or *mantra* or say a prayer of *gratitude* for special things in your life. Do a quick body scan. Do you feel lighter? Are you back in the moment? One of my spiritual teachers shared with me this advice: "Always be where your feet are." I loved the simplicity of this guidance and the clear meaning and significance of living in the moment.

Practice this calming exercise frequently throughout the day as often as possible. Whenever you are feeling a stress response or you need to make a choice between something that is going to move you toward or further away from your ideal picture, take a moment to get in touch with the present moment and how you feel.

Want More Tools?

Still struggling with overcoming feelings of self-doubt and old patterns? Again, don't be too hard on yourself. These old patterns worked, and that is why you held onto them for so long. Be gentle with yourself! Sometimes it is difficult for us to let go of something that is familiar and safe. Here is another tool to practice.

ACTIVITY 3: *Substitute you for your loved one.* Think about your problem or challenge when pondering these following questions and scenarios and record your answers or ideas in your journal.

Next step: Imagine that your child or loved one came to you with the same problem that you have now:

- What advice would you give your child?
- How would you want them to treat themselves?

Consider your thinking lately and all of the messages you have been sending yourself.

- How would you want your child to speak to him or herself?
- What advice would you give your child if he or she was talking to him or herself like that?

Who is your closest friend or family member? Think about this person and feel your love for him or her. Now consider how you are treating yourself and are feeling about your situation.

- Would you treat your best friend the way you are treating yourself?
- Why or why not?

Now apply this advice and lessons that you have learned and give yourself the same love and care that you would give your child or your closest friend or family member! By looking after yourself, you will inspire others to look after themselves!

> Happiness is when what you think, what you say, and what you do are in harmony.
>
> —Mahatma Gandhi

ACTIVITY 4: *Set yourself up for success!* Review your current behaviors to ensure that your environment is aligned with your ideal picture. Review your latest version of your evolving life purpose statement. Does anything need to be added or adjusted? Remember, this journey is a process, and new insights are emerging that will lead you toward discovering your life purpose. This exercise will help extract more information about your life purpose.

By considering the following questions, look for any gaps where new behavior could be added and older, non-effective behavior can be removed. Get your journal ready, and record any ideas as they arise.

ROUTINE

- List all of the things that you *do not like* to do in a day, a week, and a month.
- List all of the things and people who drain you.
- List all of the things you like to do but don't have enough time to do.
- What would you choose to do if you could spend your time exactly like you want?
- How would the people in your life respond?

- Imagine and describe your ideal day, right from opening your eyes to when you fall asleep!
- Thinking of all that you want to do, feel how good it is to think about this ideal day!
- Create your ideal routine now.

DIET/HEALTH

- Are you eating exactly the way you want to be eating?
- What is preventing you from eating the way you want?
- How can you add interest and variety to your diet?
- Do you have regular visits to specialists to manage your health?
- Are you stressed? What methods have you used that work in reducing your stress?

HOME

- Does my house reflect my ideal picture in my ideal life?
- What colors and textures express my personality?
- Is my house organized and clean?
- How do I feel when I enter my house? How do I want it to feel?
- What can I add to or remove from my current home to align it with my ideal picture?

ROLE MODELS/MENTORS/FRIENDS

- Name five people who inspire you. Why?
- Do you have a role model? Mentor? Best friend? What qualities do you appreciate and value in these people?
- Who are the friends who fill you up with joy and bring positive energy into your life?

- How much time do you spend with these people? How much time do you want to spend with them?
- What activities can you add to or remove from your routine to bring more energetic people into your life?

EXERCISE/WELLNESS/SPIRITUALITY

- Does your routine allocate enough time for exercise to attain your ideal picture?
- Are there any new ways you would like to express yourself physically or psychologically?
- What activities can you add to or remove from your routine to allow more time to exercise and increase your psychological wellbeing?
- Describe your spiritual beliefs and how these beliefs unfold in your life each day.
- List your values and how your behavior reflects your values.

CAREER/WORK

- Does your job reflect your ideal life?
- Imagine your ideal job and future career plan. What can you do today to move you closer to this ideal job and career?
- What is preventing you from creating the ideal work in your life?
- How much time do you commit each week to learning, networking, and preparing for receiving your ideal career?
- What can you do today to move yourself closer to this picture?

SELF-TALK/RELATIONSHIP WITH SELF

- Do you believe that you are special?
- How do you treat yourself? Do you generally speak kindly and compassionately to yourself?
- Do you celebrate alone, filling yourself up with joy regularly?
- What do you do for yourself to reward and appreciate your success?
- If you wanted to do something nice for your loved one, what would you do? You deserve the same treatment. What can you do for yourself today?

Affirmation: I deserve to receive goodness in life.

You are the only person in the entire world who has the unique combination of experiences that creates your individual perspective. No one else is exactly like you. Your life has a purpose, and people are waiting for you to share the dreams that are in your heart!

We are so much more than the behavior and words we use to limit, define, and hurt ourselves with, so even if you make a decision that moves you one step away from your picture, take another two steps forward toward it without punishing yourself!

Just keep going! Keep practicing! Your ideal life is worth working toward, and it is all here. You just have to accept it as your truth. All that you want is right here for you receive. Just keep going! Keep believing!

Anything or anyone that does not bring you alive is too small for you.

—David Whyte

Praise and blame, gain and loss, pleasure and sorrow come and go like the wind. To be happy, rest like a giant tree, in the midst of them all.

—Buddha

7. Continue to Evolve!

Embrace the change that has flowed into your life! Change is inevitable and happens regardless of how much we want to stop the process. Harness the energy of change and direct it toward your dreams. Create what you really want in your life!

By this stage, you have manifested much of what you wanted for yourself in your relationships, career, and health and wellness. Your life is more authentic, and you have practiced techniques and strategies to listen to your heart and look to your body for feedback in order to choose behaviors that are aligned with living your life purpose! Look around at what you have attracted to you, and enjoy the result of your efforts!

ACTIVITY 1: *Review the life lessons!* You have arrived, and much of what you wanted in your ideal life is now your reality! Some of what hasn't is likely on its way. Continue to believe and feel good about it! Review the following questions, and write out your response in your journal or talk about it with a friend:

- Is living your life purpose all that you imagined and expected it to be?
- How would you describe your journey to get here? Was your experience aligned with your intention?

- What were the main lessons and insights that you have learned through the process?
- Do you remember a challenge that you had to overcome during this process? How did you get past it?
- What advice would you give to someone else starting the Follow Your Heart program?
- How do you think your life is different now that you have learned the techniques of following your heart?

It is very likely that you are feeling energized and feel like the whole world has now opened up. Instead of relaxing and sinking into all of the new changes in your life, you may get here and want to ride the wave of change further. Go for it! Alternatively, you may want to rest and absorb the newness. This is your life! It is your choice to use your power to choose.

> After climbing a great hill, one only finds that there are many more hills to climb. I have taken a moment here to rest, to steal a view of the glorious vista that surrounds me, to look back on the distance I have come.
>
> —Nelson Mandela

How Do You Proceed from Here? Consult Your Heart! You Have the Answers!

Keep adding to the pictures of your ideal life! Keep expanding, developing, and utilizing your power. Create more of what you want! Wanting more does not mean that you are selfish or incapable of being satisfied; it means that you have uncovered something inside of you that wants to blossom and flourish! You have released your inner truth, and it is spreading! Don't hold back. Just follow your heart! If you get discouraged and feel that things aren't happening fast enough, consider this perspective:

People overestimate what they can do in one year but underestimate what they can do in ten.

I am deeply grateful to the person who shared this statement because of its truth. Pace yourself. Keep your eye on your goal. Live intentionally and patiently.

You can have it all. Just not all at once.

—Oprah Winfrey

ACTIVITY 2: *Develop an action plan!* Consider your vision for your future and all of the images you have collected of you living your life purpose.

- Think of all you would like to achieve in ten years. Write it down.
- Work your way backward. What would you like to experience in five years? Write it down.
- What would you like your life experience to be in three years? Write it down.
- What you like to have, be, do, or see in one year? Write it down.

Review your lists, and write down what you can do today to move yourself forward toward your ideal life. Create a list of items that you can do over the next month that will move you forward toward this dream. Then continue to write lists; this is your action plan. If you ever feel stuck, go back to this exercise and take action! Simply create a list and check off the items. Don't overcomplicate things!

For nearly two years, I was blessed to work with a professional, dynamic, intelligent woman named Claire. She desperately wanted to leave her secure corporate job for a career she was passionate about, but she was afraid. She held an image of herself working as an executive director for a not-for-profit organization. She wanted to be passionate again about her career and thought this leadership position would fulfill her dream. She saw herself speaking in front of a group, sharing and inspiring. She found a magazine photo that paralleled her vision and posted it on her vision board. Together we created an action plan from that image.

Her action plan included items such as:

- Identify which organizations' mission statements touch your heart.
- Make a list of questions you want to know about each organization, and then call them and schedule an informational interview.
- Identify the skills and qualities you have that you can share with that organization.
- Identify the gaps you have with what they need, and bridge those gaps by taking training and certification so you are competitive as an executive director.

Other action steps included improving her public speaking skills, expanding her social network, reading publications, and exploring her passions, including art history and international business. The action steps were motivating to her because they were aligned with a vision of her life purpose.

However, as Claire got closer to this goal, she realized that being an executive director was not really what she wanted. But what next? She was afraid of leaving her position but knew it was time to move on.

With the intention of following her heart, Claire identified her happy list and did a lot of work identifying all of the things that energized her.

Each day, she created new, healthy ways of living, including changes to her diet, exercise, and even the way she shared herself in relationships. She was more authentic with her husband, and they explored new leisure activities together. Life became more fun, light, and exciting. She connected with new and old friends. She said yes more instead of saying no. Slowly she became empowered and clear about her voice, and as a result, her new ideas about her life purpose emerged.

Knowing what she was passionate about and the skills she wanted to use, she clarified her vision of her career and saw herself as a consultant, working from her home office contributing her expertise at an international level. Soon after she clarified her vision further and effortlessly secured a lucrative contract and more work—and money quickly flowed in!

Claire courageously let go of her fear and said good-bye to her secure corporate position. This was a huge step for her! We would often get goose bumps and giggle at the regular synchronicity she experienced and rapid pace these new opportunities were delivered right to her. She was so clear!

She bravely let go of it all and chose in favor of her dreams.

She was surprised at how much support and encouragement she received from others and told me how one of her friends was inspired to change her career and follow her dreams as a result. It was a pivotal moment in Claire's life.

Even today as Claire's journey continues to unfold she follows her heart and is guided by the visions she has for her future. She no longer looks for her meaning or life purpose outside of herself. She turns inward for direction. Being a witness to this change in her was beyond beautiful. I am honored to have been a part of her transformation.

ACTIVITY 3: *Pray Regularly & Be humble!* Practice humility and thank God, Source or the Universe every day for the strength, faith, and courage to use the skills you were blessed with to get you to this place in your life.

Now is the perfect time while you are standing here, surrounded by all that you asked for, to say thank you. Write in your gratitude journal a prayer, mantra, or list, capturing your gratitude and how you are aware of all you have received.

You may realize that living your life purpose isn't exactly what you imagined or really what you wanted, which does happen sometimes; because what we think we want isn't really what we need. If this is you, try not to get discouraged and instead look at how you have harnessed your power and created your desires. Using what you have learned, continue to evolve, explore, and listen. Create a new vision board, immerse yourself, and align with those new images. Clarify again the intention for how you want to live your life, stating your life purpose and choosing in favor of this purpose. Be open to messages, and accept guidance all around you.

The change process is never ending. New pictures will always be entering and leaving our ideal life as we continue to discover our true potential. We always do our best with whatever information we have in that moment. Now we know better, so we will do better! Be kind to yourself. Each one of us is learning on this journey.

> Kindness in words creates confidence. Kindness in thinking creates profoundness. Kindness in giving creates love.
> —Lao-Tzu

Change can be both exhilarating and terrifying, depending on your perspective, so when fear and doubt arise, quiet them by returning to your breath, and turn your attention to the moment. Continue to practice and work with the activities presented within the Follow Your Heart program. Overcome fear, and find peace by following your heart!

Peace is its own reward.

—Mahatma Gandhi

Getting over a painful experience is much like crossing monkey bars. You have to let go at some point in order to move forward.

—Author Unknown

Conclusion

So what happens next? Because we are still alive, the journey isn't over. We have more lessons to learn, so we continue onward and inward, continuing to discover more about ourselves, each other, and our world.

Throughout this process, if we have engaged and completed the activities of the Follow Your Heart program, we have overcome our deepest fears and embraced life, expanded ourselves, and created so much of what we wanted! Change is inevitable, and once we accept this fact instead of fearing change, we can flow with it and move forward peacefully.

When you are mindful and act intentionally, you continue to evolve with each new idea and situation presented, discovering the beauty and perfection that already exists with you. You will never go backward once the lesson has really been learned. You may be tested time and again, but you have new information and tools. Therefore, your life will never be the same after this moment passes.

When I reflect on my journey since making the decision to live aligned with my life purpose, I clearly recognize the change in myself. When approaching my daily tasks instead of running to the finish line, I monitor myself and dip into the state of calmness that exists, and is offered to each of us, in every moment throughout the day.

My persistent struggle to create a feeling of security is now replaced with a deep sense of harmony and acceptance about life. And because of this shift, my relationship with time has changed. I don't judge myself harshly about what I haven't done yet or don't have yet. Instead, I luxuriously nurture myself with compassionate thoughts that flow outward from me, felt through my interactions with others and generates a sense of peace and lightness in my life.

I set daily intentions toward savoring each joyful and sensual experience in my life. I joyfully celebrate my friends and family and share my love with the world. And I don't think that this will change.

I have learned my lesson about self-care and listening to my voice and my heart. I continue to learn and grow and subsequently have new ideas and dreams. More and more continues to awaken in me, and the transformation of my life continues. I am energized and full of wonder of what is ahead!

Each one of us has a gift to share in the world and a duty to share it. The world benefits when each of us contributes our unique skills. We make an impact in the world when we live authentically; there is increased harmony and positive energy that radiates from us when we are authentic.

Living in your truth and your purpose is empowering. Bliss is the only word I can think of to express how I feel when a client has a powerful insight and then embraces his or her uniqueness and believes in his or her dreams. My gift is to see the gifts in others. My intention is to embrace the moments in my life, passionately following my heart and inspiring and empowering others to do the same. These are my final words to you:

> It is love that makes the impossible possible.
>
> —Indian Proverb

> Love is life. And if you miss love, you miss life.
>
> —Leo Buscaglia

Be in love! Love yourself. Love others. When we approach the world with love, life is magical! You have a choice! Embrace your life!

Journal

Recommended Reading

Thank you to the following authors for inspiring me and influencing my work. To my readers, I highly recommend you continue reading, learning and applying the messages in your life. Enjoy!

~

Diane Dreher, *The Tao of Inner Peace*, New York, New York: Plume Publishing, 2000.

William Glasser, M.D., *Choice Theory: A New Psychology of Personal Freedom*, New York, New York: Harper Publishing, 1998.

Miguel Angel Ruiz, M.D., *The Four Agreements: A Practical Guide to Personal Freedom, a Totlec Wisdom Book*, San Rafael, California: Amber-Allen Publishing, Inc., 1997.

Julia Cameron, *The Artist's Way: A Spiritual Path to Higher Creativity*, New York, New York: Penguin Putnam Inc., 2002.

Louise L. Hay, *You Can Heal Your Life*, Carlsbad, California: Hay House, Inc., 2004.

Bo Lozoff, *It's a Meaningful Life: It Just Takes Practice*, New York, New York: Penguin Group, 2001.

Matthew McKay, PhD and Patrick Fanning, *Self-Esteem*, Oakland, CA: New Harbinger Publications, 2000.

Jack Canfield with Janet Switzer, *The Success Principles How to Get from Where You Are to Where You Want to Be*, New York, New York: Harper Collins, 2005.

Shakti Gawain compiled by Denise Grimshaw, *Reflections in the Light—Daily Thoughts and Affirmations Revised Edition*, Novato, California: New World Library, 2003.

Eckhart Tolle, *A New Earth: Awakening to Your Life's Purpose*, New York, New York: Penguin Group, 2005.

Eckhart Tolle, *The Power of Now: A Guide to Spiritual Enlightenment*, Novato, California: Namaste Publishing and New World Library, 2004.

Jean Smith, *Breath Seeps Mind: A First Guide To Meditation Practice*, New York, New York: Riverhead Books, 1998.

Gillian Stokes, *Forgiveness: Wisdom from around the World*, London, UK: MQP Publications, 2002.

Rhonda Byrne, *The Secret*, New York, New York and Hillsboro, Oregon: Atria Books and Beyond Words Publishing, 2006.

Tara Fraser, *Yoga for You: A Step-by-Step Guide to Yoga at Home for Everybody*, London, England: Duncan Baird Publishers, 2001.

Charles Haanel, *The Master Key System: Your Step-by-Step Guide to Using the Law of Attraction*, New York, New York: Putnam, 2007.

Bruce Lipton, *Biology of Belief, Unleashing the Power Of Consciousness, Matter, and Miracles*, Carlsbad, California: Hay House Publishing Inc., 2011.

Diane Tracey, *Take This Job and Love It: Personal Guide to Career Empowerment*, New York, New York: McGraw-Hill, Inc., 1994.

Eknath Easwaran, *The Bhagavad Gita*, Tomales, California: Nilgiri Press, 2007.

Marianne Williamson, *A Return to Love: Reflections on the Principles of "A Course in Miracles,"* New York, New York: Harper Collins Publishers, 1996.

Doreen Virtue, Ph.D., *Messages from Your Angels What Your Angels Want You to Know*, Carlsbad, California: Hay House Inc., 2002.

Kelly MacLellan, M.Sc., CC—Life Coach, Author, Speaker

Kelly is a certified life and career coach and holds a master's degree in rehabilitation counseling, bachelor's degree in sociology, diploma in social services, certificates in human resources, choice theory and reality therapy, and other professional development courses. She has over twelve years of professional experience working directly with individuals to facilitate action toward their employment and life goals. Kelly is a member of the International Coaching Federation and has completed the life and career coaching certificates through the Life Purpose Institute and also the Law of Attraction Coaching program through Jack Canfield's coaching organization.

In 2007, Kelly changed her life, faced her deepest fears, developed new personal truths, followed her dreams of living in the sun, and moved to the Caribbean! Kelly leads by example and follows her heart, approaching each day with wonderment. She spends her time with family and friends, volunteering, writing, deepening her spiritual practice, learning Spanish, and guiding others through her coaching business, Embrace Your Life Coaching.

As a life coach, she creates a safe place for her clients to open their hearts and share their stories and dreams, closely listening, and then gently guides them through the Follow Your Heart Program to identify their life purpose. She shares her knowledge of how to create an authentic and fulfilling life lovingly with others. She offers worldwide phone/Skype consultations on how to embrace your divine gifts and follow the path of your heart to the life of your dreams. Kelly specializes in discovering life purposes, creating action plans, overcoming barriers, improving self-awareness, and releasing your fear so you can realize your true potential.

Connect with Kelly at her website and blog at www.embraceyourlife.ca.

Kelly lives in Ontario, Canada with her husband and daughter.

Let's Connect:

Twitter: KellyMacLellan1
Facebook: Kelly MacLellan
LinkedIn: Kelly MacLellan MSc
E-mail: Kelly@embraceyourlife.ca